WALKING IN MADEIRA

Looking along the cliffs of the north coast, halfway through Walk 9

WALKING IN MADEIRA

by

Paddy Dillon

2 POLICE SQUARE, MILNTHORPE, CUMBRIA, LA7 7PY
www.cicerone.co.uk

© Paddy Dillon 2002
ISBN 1 85284 334 9
Reprinted 2004
A catalogue record for this book is available from the British Library

ABOUT THE AUTHOR

Paddy Dillon is a prolific outdoor writer with a score and more books to his name, as well as a dozen booklets and brochures. He writes for a number of outdoor magazines and other publications, as well as producing materials for tourism groups and other organisations. He lives on the fringe of the Lake District, and has walked, and written about walking, in every county in England, Scotland, Ireland and Wales. He generally leads at least one guided walking holiday overseas every year and has walked in many parts of Europe, as well as Nepal, Tibet and the Canadian Rockies.

While walking his routes, Paddy inputs his notes directly into a palm-top computer every few steps. His descriptions are therefore precise, having been written at the very point at which the reader uses them. He takes all his own photographs and often draws his own maps to illustrate his routes. He has appeared on television, and is a member of the Outdoor Writers' Guild.

Cicerone guides by Paddy Dillon:

Irish Coastal Walks

The Irish Coast to Coast

The Mountains of Ireland

Channel Island Walks

The Isles of Scilly

Walking in the Isle of Arran

Walking the Galloway Hills

Walking in County Durham

Walking the North Pennines

GR20 Corsica: High Level Route

Walking in the Canary Islands – Volume 1

Walking in the Canary Islands – Volume 2

Walking in Malta

Front cover: The path from Pico do Areeiro to Pico Ruivo (Walk 12)

CONTENTS

Advice to Readers

Readers are advised that while every effort is taken by the author to ensure the accuracy of this guidebook, changes can occur which may affect the contents. It is advisable to check locally on transport, accommodation, shops, etc, but even rights of way can be altered.

The publisher would welcome notes of any such changes.

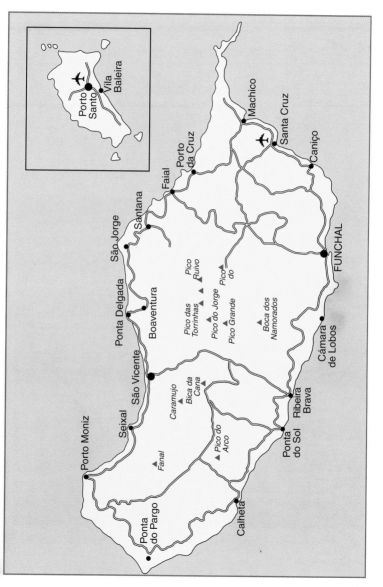

Porto Santo
Vila Baleira

Porto Moniz
Seixal
São Vicente
Ponta Delgada
São Jorge
Santana
Faial
Porto da Cruz
Machico
Santa Cruz
Caniço
FUNCHAL
Câmara de Lobos
Ribeira Brava
Ponta do Sol
Calheta
Ponta do Pargo
Boaventura

Fanal
Caramujo
Bica da Cana
Pico do Arco
Pico das Torrinhas
Pico do Jorge
Pico Grande
Pico Ruivo
Pico do
Boca dos Namorados

A view from the Levada do Curral up through the valley to the peaks, Walk 38

Introduction

Madeira rises steep and rocky from the Atlantic Ocean off the coasts of Europe and Africa. It stands in splendid isolation and the nearest island groups are the distant Azores and Canary Islands. Madeira enjoys a subtropical climate that many walkers would find acceptable throughout the year. As a compact and mountainous island, criss-crossed by a network of old paths and tracks, it is remarkably scenic and accessible. Water is conveyed round the island in charming flower-fringed channels called 'levadas', which offer anything from a gentle stroll to seriously exposed cliff walks. There are wooded valleys, rocky slopes, cultivated terraces and impressive cliff coasts to explore. This guidebook includes a rich and varied selection of walks on Madeira, and includes a couple of walks on the neighbouring island of Porto Santo.

LOCATION

Madeira is a small island of around 750km² (290 square miles). It lies at 32°46′N / 17°03′W in the subtropical Atlantic Ocean, about 600km (370 miles) from Morocco in North Africa, and about 950km (590 miles) from Portugal, to which it belongs. Its closest neighbours include Porto Santo, about 40km (25 miles) away, and the Ilhas Desertas, about 20km (13 miles) from

Looking back along the jagged cliffs of the Ponta de São Lourenço, Walk 11

Madeira at their closest point. Other island groups are far from view, such as the Azores and Canary Islands, to which Madeira is loosely associated by reason of lying along the same huge fracture in the earth's crust.

GEOLOGY

Madeira is essentially a volcanic island, though volcanic activity has long ceased. Magma from deep within the earth spewed out onto the ocean floor around 130 million years ago. Gradually, enough material built up for

The houses of Curral das Freiras spill down the steep valley sides, Walk 18

land to appear above the water, so that Madeira was born about 2½ million years ago. Some corals managed to establish themselves around the fringe of the new island, and these are preserved in small locations as fossils. The overwhelming bulk of the island, however, is made up of basaltic lava flows shot through with doleritic dykes. It is thought that volcanic activity ceased around 25,000 years ago. The nearby island of Porto Santo, incidentally, is older than Madeira. Although mostly basaltic like its larger neighbour, Porto Santo also has a central band of calcareous sandstone that produces a fertile soil and has eroded to form a magnificent sandy beach.

DISCOVERY AND HISTORY

Although the true story of Madeira's discovery may never be known, early records agree that it was a densely wooded and uninhabited island. Fanciful tales of Madeira's discovery do not tie in too easily with the rather scant historical documentation. It certainly is not a remnant of the fabled Atlantis. Some early maps show the island and there is a suspicion that the Phoenicians may have been the first to set eyes on Madeira. Others say the Genoans discovered the place. Some records state that the Spaniards were in the habit of stopping off at Porto Santo on trips between Spain and the Canary Islands. A strange story relates how an Englishman, along with his wife and a companion, were marooned on Madeira, and thus became the first, albeit temporary settlers.

Reliable records of discovery and settlement start from 1418. Prince Henry 'The Navigator' of Portugal patronised voyages to seek new territories. João Goncalves Zarco was leading one of these voyages around Africa in 1419, when he was blown off-course and landed on Porto Santo. In 1420, while checking out possibilities for settling the island, he also discovered Madeira. By 1425 great fires were started to clear Madeira's native woodlands and open up some of the slopes for settlement and cultivation. In 1452 slaves were drafted in to work the land and dig a network of irrigation channels, or 'levadas'. In 1478 it is said that Christopher Columbus visited Madeira and Porto Santo, and was convinced that by sailing ever westwards he would find a route to India. He later discovered the Americas.

The position of Madeira and Porto Santo, rather remote from mother Portugal, left it open to attack by pirates from Europe and Africa. The islands suffered several raids, resulting in the destruction of property, looting, and the capture and killing of island inhabitants. Fortifications were constructed, such as a wall around Funchal in 1542, but most of the island communities were unprotected. In calmer times, the islands enjoyed good trade links and continued to develop their agriculture, making a particular feature of their fine wines. By 1662, following a marriage between Charles II of England and Catherine of Braganza, English merchants settled on Madeira and took key positions in the wine trade.

By 1807 English troops were stationed in Madeira as Napoleon conquered more and more parts of Europe. In more settled times, in the 1850s, cholera wiped out thousands of islanders, while disease destroyed the vines. Around this time, banana cultivation began to develop more intensively.

Tourism has developed since 1890, the climate of the islands making it a favourite winter destination for richer Europeans. Although Portugal was neutral in the war years, it suffered under a dictatorship and many Madeirans seized the chance to emigrate to other parts of Europe, or to Angola, Brazil or Venezuela. Madeira has been an autonomous region since 1976, and following Portugal's entry into the EU, vast sums of money have been applied to developing Madeira's infrastructure. Tourism continues to boom and walking is an important pursuit for many visitors. Fortunately, for a relatively small island, there are plenty of opportunities to explore on foot.

WEATHER

In a nutshell, Madeira is hot and humid. It is an all-year-round destination, but the summer months could be rather too hot for some people, and there is a risk of snowfall and cold winds in the mountains in winter. Some parts of the island may look dry, but on the whole it is a remarkably green and well-watered place. The water has to come from somewhere. A typical Madeiran day starts sunny and clear.

Afternoon clouds begin to drift across the high peaks of Madeira, Walk 14

During the afternoon, clouds begin to wreathe themselves around the peaks and may completely blanket the mountains later. In the evening the cloud may break up again, but not before the mist has dampened the 'cloud forest' on the high northern slopes of the island. Generally, the greater the altitude, the more likely there is to be cool air, mist and light rain, but it is seldom so severe as to force walkers into retreat, and often enough it is sunny and clear all day long. Be warned that this is a subtropical island, and depending on the direction of the wind and the amount of moisture it carries, there can occasionally be prolonged or torrential rain. The ground tends to allow an immediate run-off, but vast amounts of water soak into the ground and are stored in the bedrock, so many rivers are able to run throughout the year.

LANDSCAPE

Madeira's landscape is one of exceptional beauty and ruggedness. The first thing visitors notice are the steep slopes. Between the airport and Funchal these slopes are well settled and dotted with bright, white buildings. However, there are plenty of trees and shrubs along with a splendid array of colourful flowers. Bananas and palms jostle with bird of paradise flowers and amaryllis, while further uphill are stands of pine and eucalyptus. Exploring beyond Funchal, there are quiet wooded valleys with exceptionally steep and rugged slopes, and treeless mountains at a higher level. Always, the steepness of the slopes is apparent, and anyone exploring on foot will need to find acceptable routes and gradients! On the northern side of Madeira there are damp and green 'cloud forest' and 'laurisilva' woodlands. Water is abundant here, but in many places it is siphoned off along 'levada' channels, through awesome rock tunnels beneath the mountains, either to generate power or to irrigate the cultivation terraces on the southern slopes of Madeira. The roads, tracks and paths that lead through the landscape twist and turn so much that they present ever-changing outlooks on the scenery. Variety is one of the great charms of the island, and there is plenty of variety beside the levadas, through the wooded valleys, over the mountain tracks and along the rugged coastal paths.

LANGUAGE

Madeira's language is naturally Portuguese, and if you have any proficiency in that tongue you will notice that Madeirans have their own accent and colloquialisms. Sometimes the origin of certain placenames has been lost. It is useful to learn enough key phrases to negotiate a bus journey or ask for basic directions, but it is also true that many young Madeirans have a good grasp of English and other

A typical early morning mountain view from Pico do Areeiro, Walk 12

Topographical glossary

achada	hillside plateau
água	water
alto	high
baixo	low
boca	col/gap/saddle
caldeirão	cauldron/hollow
caminho	road
campo	field
curral	valley
da/de/do/das/	
dos	of the
fajã	flat land
fonte	spring/fountain
grande	big/large
igreja	church
levada	watercourse
lombo	ridge/crest
miradouro	viewpoint
nova	new
paragem	bus stop
pequena	little/small
pico	peak
ponta	point
porto	port/harbour
Posto Florestal	forestry post
praia	beach
quinta	farm/big house
ribeira/ribeiro	river
santo/são	saint
vale	valley
velha	old
vereda	path

languages, and the mix of visitors makes the island seem quite cosmopolitan. While using a map, it is useful to know what some of the placenames refer to, so consult the list below for a few commonly used terms. Don't be afraid to practise a few words of Portuguese. No matter how bad you think you sound, be assured that the Madeirans have heard plenty of really bad pronunciation and yours is unlikely to be the worst!

ISLAND TREES AND FLOWERS

From the moment Madeira rose from the ocean, some attempt will have been made by terrestrial plants to gain a roothold. Maybe lichens and mosses managed to eke out an existence in tiny crevices, sometimes thriving, then being overwhelmed by lava flows. Later, a variety of plants, including flowers and trees, will have become established. When Madeira was first discovered, it was referred to as a well-wooded island, and rather unusually, most of the trees belonged to the laurel family. Neighbouring Porto Santo was famous for its 'dragon trees'. The first seeds to reach these islands could have been deposited on the shore after floating on the ocean currents, or they could have been borne on the wind or deposited in bird droppings. No-one will ever know for sure.

Madeira is said to have the largest 'laurisilva', or wild laurel forest, in the world. It features the mighty til tree, bay tree and Madeira mahogany. There are also delightful lily of the valley trees and intriguing wax myrtles, or candleberry trees. Vast areas of the higher mountains are covered in ancient, gnarled tree heather, with tall bilberry alongside. Walkers who are used to trampling on heather and bilberry may be surprised to find it grows so densely that it blocks the sunlight! Large open areas are covered in the ubiquitous bracken. On the northern slopes the tree cover is termed 'cloud forest' as it draws much of its moisture from the

Wooded and cultivated slopes crossed by the Levada dos Tornos, Walk 2

mist or fine drizzle that hogs the heights. The 'cloud forest' is also rich in ferns, mosses and liverworts. Some of the ferns are endemic to Madeira and in some parts of the world are known only from fossil records.

The bird of paradise flower is Madeira's national flower, and other famous species include the pride of Madeira and the amaryllis. Listing the endemic flora of Madeira would take some time, and entire books have been written on the subject. There are about 200 species that are indigenous to Madeira, the Azores, Canary Islands and Cabo Verde Islands, and about 120 of these are endemic in Madeira. Add to this the number of plants that have been introduced to Madeira, or grow in gardens, or are under cultivation, and the species count becomes quite bewildering. Non-native flowers include the soil-binding agapanthus that flourishes alongside so many of the 'levadas'.

Non-native trees include eucalyptus, mimosa and acacia, though there are efforts to control the spread of these into the native 'laurisilva'. Vines are grown on some of the lower, sunny slopes, and huge areas are planted with dwarf bananas. All kinds of fruit and vegetables are grown on terraces that have been laboriously hacked from the mountainsides. Longstanding gardens and parks are planted with all manner of exotic trees, shrubs and flowers. In some of the parks cared for by the island authorities, many of the trees and shrubs are labelled, enabling comparisons to be made with anything found growing wild.

To delve more deeply into Madeira's wonderfully extensive and complex flora, be sure to visit some of the botanical gardens, and carry a copy of *The Plants and Flowers of Madeira* by António da Costa and Luis de O Franquinho.

ISLAND BIRDS

The only creatures that could reach the new island of Madeira had to fly, including insects, bats and birds. While the species count is low, and some species are becoming alarmingly scarce, there are a few birds that are endemic to the island. Perhaps the most famous is the long-toed pigeon, which lives in the most secluded parts of the 'laurisilva'. Other birds include the tiny firecrest, the smallest of Madeira's birds, as well as Madeiran varieties of chaffinch, grey wagtail, pipit and rock sparrow. Perhaps the most infrequently spotted bird is the Madeiran storm petrel, which spends most of its time far out to sea.

ISLAND ANIMALS

Land animals did not make it to Madeira under their own volition. A variety of seal known as a 'sea wolf' made its home on these shores, feeding from the fish in the waters around the island. They are confined to the Ilhas Desertas these days. Dolphins and whales also pass these islands. There is a whale museum at Caniçal for those with an interest in whales, and there are echoes of the epic tale of 'Moby Dick'. Lizards are common in almost every sunny spot.

During the settlement of Porto Santo and Madeira, animals were brought onto the islands. Porto Santo suffered a devastating plague of rabbits that ate everything the settlers tried to grow! The land on Porto Santo is now largely used for cattle grazing, though it looks dry and barren. In Madeira, livestock are rarely seen in the open, but there are cattle, sheep, goats and pigs. Animals are often kept indoors rather than grazed outdoors, so farmers are often seen carrying huge bundles of fodder or bedding for their animals.

THE NATIONAL PARK

Much of the central and high ground in Madeira is designated as the 'Parque Natural da Madeira'. It includes virtually all the wild, uninhabited and uncultivated areas. The few buildings in these parts are generally owned by the government, such as the Forestry Posts or 'Posto Florestal'. Of prime importance is the conservation of the remaining 'laurisilva' woodlands as a living ecosystem. There are special areas of note, such as Fanal with its huge, ancient til trees; the Parque Ecológico do Funchal, where native trees are being replanted; the Ponta de São Lourenço, where flowers are being conserved; and the Ilhas Desertas, which are rich in birdlife. There is a marine reserve called the 'Reserva Natural Parcial do Garajau'. Walkers should tread circumspectly in all these special areas and cause as little disturbance to the flora and fauna as possible.

Water pours into a pool from a number of springs at 25 Fontes, Walk 30

GETTING TO MADEIRA

Madeira is a popular package holiday destination. Flights are mainly chartered and holiday reps abound at the airport to deal with their clients. Visitors are loaded onto buses and taken to their hotels, with their baggage in hot pursuit. It may look chaotic at times, but the system seems to work well enough. When you leave Madeira, it's usual for the companies to get you to the airport well in advance of your flight, so expect a delay of sorts on departure.

If you try to organise a flight-only deal, you'll actually be issued with a basic accommodation voucher, as all visitors to the island must have some sort of pre-booked accommodation. The bulk of accommodation is in the 'Hotel Zone' to the west of Funchal, though there are hotels and apartments dotted all around the island. There are only two camp sites; one on Madeira at Porto Moniz and one on Porto Santo. True budget accommodation is virtually absent from the islands.

Almost every European country offers charter flights to Madeira, though the colder North European countries seem to offer more choices. The usual charter deals run from Monday to Monday, for one or two weeks. It's possible to secure three or four weeks, or even longer, though it's necessary to search longer to find an appropriate deal. The choice is bewildering, as there are so many operators offering holiday deals, so shop around to find a flight and accommodation at a suitable price. Flight prices start as low as £99 and even when packaged with accommodation for a week may still be less than £250. An extra week shouldn't cost a whole lot more, but it depends on where you stay and whether you book a full meals service or opt for self-catering. Travel agents, newspapers and magazines often feature holiday deals to Madeira throughout the year, so keep your eyes peeled for one that's right for you.

There have always been close ties between the UK and Madeira. Charter flights are offered by UK companies such as Airtours, Air 2000, JMC and Thomsons. UK airports with charter flights to Funchal include Birmingham, Gatwick, Glasgow, Luton, Manchester and Newcastle. In the winter months additional airports may include Bournemouth, Bristol and Stanstead.

Scheduled flights are operated by British Airways from Gatwick and TAP (Air Portugal) from Heathrow. There is the option of flying direct to Funchal or flying via Lisbon in Portugal. The only real benefit with a scheduled flight is that you have more flexibility over your choice of dates, usually at a higher price. TAP seems to overbook seats rather enthusiastically, so if you choose to fly with them, be prepared to be the one who gets bumped onto a later flight! TAP also operates 15 minute flights between Madeira and Porto Santo. Sometimes these are fully booked, but when there are seats available, it's possible to turn up at either airport and book a flight as easily as you would catch a bus.

A view of Madeira's high peaks from the early stages of the old road, Walk 47

Although most European countries have relatively easy air access to Madeira, anyone flying from the United States or the rest of the world would be better arranging a connecting scheduled flight via Heathrow, Gatwick or Lisbon. Non-Europeans should also check current visa requirements, though even Europeans will have to produce passports or identity cards.

Although Madeira's Santa Caterina runway has been vastly extended, it's still not without problems. Wind speed and direction can make landings hazardous, and the airport is frequently closed for short periods. When this happens and a dozen flights are converging on the island, they have to make alternative landing arrangements. Sometimes a few aircraft can be accommodated at the airport on neighbouring Porto Santo. Other flights may divert to Lisbon, or even to the Canary Islands, most notably Tenerife. There's little you can do if this happens except to try and enjoy the extra hour or so in the air, and make the most of whatever arrangements are made to get you to Madeira when conditions improve. If you have to spend a night on Porto Santo when it wasn't originally on your itinerary, then count it as a bonus!

It may seem strange for an island, but there are no regular ferry services, except for the one plying between Madeira and Porto Santo. Cruise ships berth on a regular basis, including many of the big-name luxury ships, while travelling in circuits that may include the Canary Islands and West Africa.

GETTING ROUND MADEIRA

Car Hire

You can hire a car and collect it from the airport, or have it delivered to your accommodation. Until the true nature of Madeira's roads is experienced, hiring a car is not recommended. The roads are often steep and tortuous, pretty narrow in places, with plenty of blind bends and the danger of rockfalls. Better to use the buses at first and let the driver worry about the road, then consider at a later date whether to hire a car. It is true that a few of the walks are more easily accessible with a car. It is also true that driving a car requires so much concentration that you miss all the wonderful scenery along the way!

Bus Services

Madeira has a pretty comprehensive and remarkably cheap network of bus services. These are densely concentrated around Funchal, but there are companies providing vital lifelines to distant villages. To use the buses, obtain the 'Madeira by Bus' timetable booklet from the tourist information office, and pick up a free leaflet showing all the Funchal bus services. Study them carefully, taking particular note of times and destinations. Tickets can be bought on the buses, but be sure where you can join and leave services. Generally, bus stops are marked by a sign reading 'paragem', but sometimes on the country roads the bus stop is marked by a couple of yellow lines painted on the road, and are not so obvious. Note that services are reduced over the weekends, and that some 'feriados', or holidays, are covered only by Sunday timetables.

Funchal Bus

Funchal and its immediate surroundings is particularly well served by buses. They are orange, operated by Horários do Funchal, and are referred to as 'Funchal Bus' in this book. Nearly all these buses depart from bus stops that are arranged along the level coastal road called the Avenida do Mar. There are a couple of information kiosks along the road offering leaflet plans of all the city bus routes, and timetables can be checked at the appropriate stops. Either pay on board these buses, or make an advance purchase of cheaper 'two journey' tickets for the three zones that the network covers around Funchal.

Camacha Bus

Some of the more far-flung suburbs of Funchal, and places such as Camacha, Santo da Serra, Santa Cruz and Curral das Freiras, are served by Autocarros da Camacha buses. These are simply termed 'Camacha Bus' in this book. They are actually operated by the Horarios do Funchal bus company, but under a different name, and with their own ticket system. Timetable details are found on the same leaflet plan as the Funchal Bus services.

SAM Bus

The Sociedade de Automóveis da Madeira, or 'SAM Bus' in this book, serves all points between Funchal and the eastern end of Madeira. There is

Walkers on the easy path from Pico Ruivo to Achada do Teixeira, Walk 44

some overlapping with the Camacha Bus services around Santa Cruz and Santo da Serra. Other places that are served include Machico, Caniçal, Maroços, Portela, Porto da Cruz and Faial. Sometimes the Caniçal bus will continue out onto the Ponta de São Lourenço.

São Roque Bus

The São Roque do Faial bus company, referred to as 'São Roque Bus' in this book, serves several points northwards from Funchal. Places served include small towns and villages such as Poiso, Ribeiro Frio, Faial, Santana, São Jorge, Boaventura and São Vicente.

Rodoeste Bus

The Rodoeste bus company, or 'Rodoeste Bus' in this book, serves the whole western half of Madeira. There are a range of services west of Funchal, covering most villages on the way to Ribeira Brava. Beyond that point, buses make a loop taking in the Boca da Encumeada, São Vicente, Seixal, Porto Moniz, Ponta do Pargo, Prazéres, Calheta and Ponta do Sol. The western loop offers a tour around half of Madeira at a fraction of the normal tour price!

Tour Buses

There are some places where regular bus services do not operate. There are good roads to prodigious heights, such as to Pico do Areeiro, Madeira's second-highest mountain, or across the high plateau of Paúl da Serra. Some of the big tour buses run to those places and in desperation you could use them and then 'jump ship' and start walking. There is also the 'Nova' minibus service, which is geared to collecting walkers and dropping them off in out-of-the-way places. If you use the 'Nova' minibus, you'll be collected from your accommodation, dropped off at the start of a particular walk, and collected later. Current 'Nova' minibus leaflets can be obtained from the tourist information office.

Taxis

To move faster than the buses, or reach a particularly remote or awkward location, consider hiring a taxi. Taxi drivers will take you anywhere – at the right price! Although they have a recommended table of fares for long-distance runs, it is possible to negotiate a better deal. Taxis are always bright yellow with a blue stripe, generally Mercedes, though sometimes minibuses, with a meter and scale of charges. Many taxi drivers are happy to run day tours round the island, and if you want to be dropped off somewhere to walk, then be collected later, they may apply their full-day charge and throw in a mini-tour with commentary too. If you see a taxi in a remote location and want a lift, simply flag down the driver. Even if the car is full, a message could be relayed to another driver.

Helicopter

For some time there has been a helicopter for hire on Madeira, parked down by the harbour in Funchal. To see the island from the air and check out some of the more remote walking locations, then this is a possibility. Charges are literally sky-high and time in the air is limited. Telephone for details on Funchal 232882.

Ferry

To visit the neighbouring island of Porto Santo, use the Porto Santo Line ferry. This generally offers a daily service, and if you want to stay for a couple of nights, then a ferry and accommodation package can be arranged. The Porto Santo Line, or other tour operators in Funchal, can organise such a package. On a simple day-trip to Porto Santo, time for walking is limited to only a few hours, so take careful note of the timetable.

ACCOMMODATION

Broadly speaking, accommodation in Madeira is concentrated around the 'Hotel Zone' to the west of Funchal, where large hotels and apartment blocks house most of the island's visitors. There are plenty of smaller hotels scattered around the island. A large hotel complex has been built at Garajau, but most other hotel developments around the island tend to be small scale. Walkers looking for smaller or simpler places to stay will find the choice limited. In Funchal, try a bed-and-breakfast called Trejuno, halfway to Monte at Livramento. There is also the Pousada dos Vinháticos above Serra de Água. In the high mountains, there is the Pousada Areeiro on top of Pico do Areeiro. A refuge almost on the summit of Pico Ruivo offers hostel-style accommodation. Camping is limited to one campsite on Madeira at Porto Moniz and another at Vila Baleira on Porto Santo. If you really want to camp in the wilds, you are supposed to apply for a permit, though in practice few people do, and there are a number of regularly used pitches in the wilds. The drawback to backpacking in Madeira is the heat and humidity.

Anyone falling in love with Madeira and wanting to buy a property will be overwhelmed with advice. There are houses and villas for sale, as well as apartments for sale or available as timeshares. Be very firm if you come across a really pushy timeshare salesman!

TOURIST INFORMATION OFFICE

The main tourist information office in Madeira is located fairly centrally in Funchal at Avenida Arriaga 18, and is usually open from 0900 to 2000 Monday to Friday and 0900 to 1800 on Saturday. Staff speak English and they can assist with any queries about accommodation, transport, tours and visitor attractions.

MAPS OF MADEIRA

Maps of a quality similar to Ordnance Survey Landranger and Explorer maps of Britain are not available on Madeira. The Portuguese equivalent of the Ordnance Survey is the 'Serviço Cartográfico do Exército'. They produce the 1:25,000 scale 'Carta Militar' or Military Maps of Madeira, which cover the island in nine sheets. There is also the 'Instituto Geográfico e Cadastral' (IGC) that produces the 1:50,000 scale 'Ilha da Madeira' maps in two sheets. Contouring on both these series is good, and most landscape features are clear, but they tend to be out of date in terms of new roads and developments. Some of the 'levadas' are badly drawn (water does not flow uphill!) and some of the paths shown may be impassable. If you like OS style maps, these are the best that are available.

Other maps of Madeira tend to be rather 'touristy'. They make more of an attempt to show new roads and developments, but also copy errors from the Military Maps. Contouring is vague, and while most maps attempt to show some of the walking routes, it is all rather hit-and-miss. Some routes are shown dangerously out-of-line. Try the Freytag and Berndt 1:50,000 map of Madeira. The scale on this map is wrong; it is closer to 1:55,000. There is also the 1:40,000 Madeira Tour and Trail Map, published by Discovery Walking Guides.

The maps quoted in this guidebook are the Military Maps and IGC Maps of Madeira. To use these, order them well in advance from map suppliers such as Stanfords (12–14 Long Acre, London WC2E 9BR, tel 0207 836 1321), The Map Shop (15 High Street, Upton-upon-Severn WR8 0HJ, tel 01684 593146), or Cordee (3a De Montfort Street, Leicester LE1 7HD, tel 0116 254 3579). Simpler maps of Madeira and free tourist maps can be obtained on reaching the island.

The sketch maps in this book are simply for reference. Transfer details from them to whatever maps are chosen, then use the route descriptions alongside while actually walking. To aid orientation, key landmark features on the sketch maps are highlighted in bold print in the walk descriptions.

FUNCHAL AND MONTE

It is a good idea to familiarise yourself with Funchal. It is a big and bustling town, which some would even call a city, and it is where most buses, taxis and other services are to be found. If you are travelling by bus, be sure how the buses operate and where the appropriate bus stops are for the Funchal Bus services and all the other bus companies. Get a free town plan from the tourist information office and carry it whenever you are in Funchal. Basically, the town is in three parts: the Hotel Zone, the Town Centre and the Old Town, working from west to east.

Places of interest around Funchal include the Parque de Santa Catarina and Jardim Municipal, where exotic trees and flowers can be studied for free. There are plenty of shops selling wine, embroidery and souvenirs specific to the island, as well as flower-sellers on the streets. To check out the wine trade, start at the Madeira Wine Company at Avenida Arriaga 28. If you are looking for books in English, or IGC maps of Madeira (but not the Military Maps), visit the English Bookshop at Rua de Carreira 43. The town centre is always busy and bustling, but there are a number of quieter pedestrianised streets and squares. There are gardens that charge an admission fee, including the Jardim Botânico and Jardim Orquídea. Museums focus on topics as diverse as history, natural history, contemporary art, sacred art, photography, electricity and sugar! There are plenty of church sites to visit, from the central cathedral to the secluded English church. The fort on the Avenida do Mar is the seat of the regional government, and looking along the coast towards the Old Town, the fort of São Tiago can be seen. The Old Town is quite atmospheric, with narrow streets, crumbling buildings and a fairly relaxed air.

Sooner or later, all who explore Funchal turn their sights uphill to Monte. Walking up the steep roads to Monte is not recommended. They are too steep to be enjoyable, especially in the heat and humidity. Bus services run quickly and cheaply from Funchal to Monte, or there is an expensive cablecar ride from the sea. Attractions include a fine church above a leafy, shady square, and the botanical garden called the Jardim do Monte Palace. The most expensive and unusual way back to Funchal is to ride in a wicker basket known as a 'toboggan' and let a couple of men pull you down the steep road into town!

A view of Funchal rising steeply towards the mountains

THE PLAN OF THIS GUIDE

This guidebook opens with a few fairly easy 'levada' walks. They are level and have generally obvious features to follow, as well as offering good shade from the sun. Bus links are easy to use and there are plenty of services. Cautious walkers should start with these walks before progressing to the longer, more difficult, remote or exposed 'levada' walks. Be sure to read the descriptions carefully to discover how easy or difficult the walks are. Some of the later 'levada' walks could also be classed as mountain walks, but still follow the 'running theme' of water, even while grappling with exposed rocky slopes. Some more recently constructed 'levadas' include long tunnels, for which a good torch is required.

The mountain walks are generally more serious, and often follow steep and rocky paths, or very exposed ledges cut across cliff faces. In hot and humid conditions, or when the weather high in the mountains turns suddenly cold and wet, some of the routes can become quite difficult. Heavy rain brings an increased risk of rockfalls and landslides, but be warned that dangers such as these are ever-present on the island. Generally, fairly clear paths are used, but sometimes the paths are vague or the slope may be without a path altogether. In mist take great care with route-finding. There are also a few rugged coastal walks included in the book, as well as walks on the nearby island of Porto Santo.

All these walks are essentially day walks, though many of them can be linked end-to-end, or intersect with other walks, so it is possible to construct alternative walks and much longer walks. There is nothing to stop you planning a long distance 'levada' walk from west to east through Madeira, or aiming to follow the high mountain crests and ridges of Madeira from end to end, but because of the heat and humidity, very few walkers attempt serious long distance back-packing trips on the island.

Each walk opens with a brief description, then has details relating to the length of the walk, start and finishing points, maps to use, nature of the terrain, bus services and refreshments. The route descriptions lead step by step along each of the routes. Carry good maps, a compass and up-to-date bus timetables, then pace yourself to ensure that you reach the appropriate bus stop or pick-up point on time. The more remote or difficult the walk is, the more self-sufficient you need to be. Take enough food and water to drink, and try not to walk too long in open sun without taking a break in the shade. Use sunscreen, a sunhat and long-sleeved clothing to prevent sunburn. A torch is essential if the chosen walk includes long tunnels, and there is no harm in carrying spare batteries, a spare bulb, or even a spare torch.

Very few of the walks are circular, so using a car is a handicap when faced with so many linear walks. In deference to the steepness of the slopes, the heat and humidity, walks are often downhill rather than uphill. However, there are

Rugged cliffs and coves are seen on the ascent of Pico Branco, Walk 50

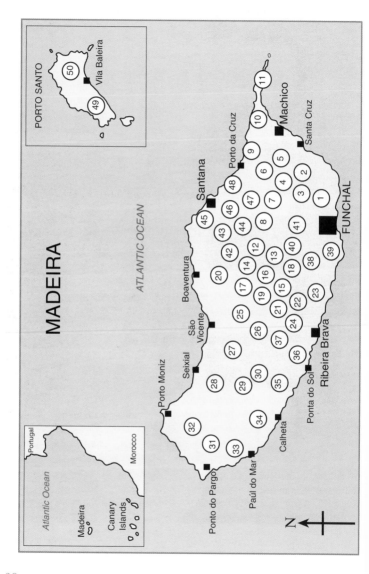

Walk 25 – The Levada do Serra pours as a waterfall on the descent to the road

exceptions, and some walks are like roller-coasters with several ascents and descents. Again, cautious walkers should start with some of the easier 'levada' walks before attempting anything too strenuous in the mountains. Bear in mind that Madeira has no organised mountain rescue service. If you need assistance, it could be a combination of the ambulance, fire service or police involved in your rescue. All three services are contacted at the same emergency telephone number, which is 115.

29

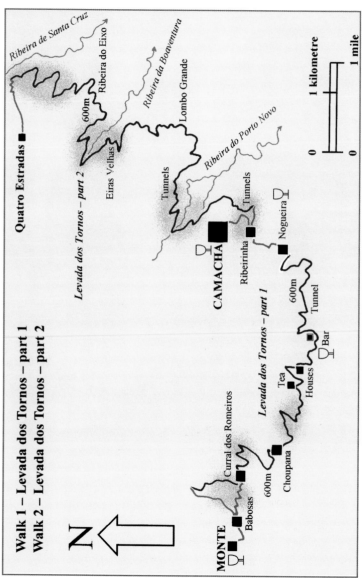

Walk 1 – Levada dos Tornos – part 1
Walk 2 – Levada dos Tornos – part 2

Walk 1: Levada dos Tornos – part 1

THE ROUTE

Distance:
16km (10 miles).

Start:
At the square at Monte – 219167.

Finish:
In the middle of Camacha – 273170.

Maps:
Military Survey 1:25,000 Sheet 9 or IGC 1:50,000
Madeira East.

Terrain:
Mostly level walking on wooded or cultivated slopes.
Some short exposed stretches and some rugged paths.
There is an optional tunnel walk.

Start at the bus terminus at **Monte**, where a cobbled square is used as a car park and taxi rank. Tall plane trees offer shade and stalls sell souvenirs. The Snack Bar Alto Monte and Café do Parque are located here, with toilets in between. There is a candle-lit shrine on the square and the Caminho Padre José Marques Jardim rises steep and cobbled, signposted for the church. It leads quickly up to the imposing building. Enjoy the view from the terrace in front of the church, then walk down the steps and turn left and right, to pass the Belomonte Restaurante Snack Bar. Turn left to follow a level, cobbled road away from Monte. Pass the entrance to the Jardim Tropical Monte Palace and follow the road past the cablecar station. Further along is a bus stop and little chapel at **Babosas.** It is a shady spot with benches beneath tall plane trees, and a viewpoint overlooks a steep, wooded valley.

Follow the cobbled track called the Caminho Rev Padre Eugénio Borgonovo, signposted for the Levada dos

The Levada dos Tornos carries water from north to south through Madeira. In the north the water is largely confined to tunnels, so it is only really possible to walk the southern parts of the levada. There is about 27km (16¼ miles) of walkable path on the southern stretch, and most walkers are happy to complete that over two days. The general altitude is 600m (1970ft). This first stretch runs from Monte to Camacha and is a fine introduction to 'levada' walking, with a couple of tea houses and bars for refreshment. An exposed stretch near the beginning and a tunnel in the middle are optional.

Transport:
Funchal Bus 20, 21 and
48 serve Monte. There is
also a cablecar from
Funchal to Monte.
Funchal Bus 22 serves
Babosas. Funchal Bus 29
serves Curral dos
Romeiros. Funchal Bus
47 serves Hortensia
Gardens Tea House and
Jasmin Tea House.
Camacha Bus 110 serves
Nogueira. Camacha Bus
29, 77 and 110 serve
Camacha. Taxis at Monte
and Camacha.

Refreshments:
Snack bars and cafés at
Monte. Hortensia
Garden Tea House and
Jasmin Tea House round
Lombo da Quinta.
Pastelaria Candeeiro
snack bar above
Nogueira. A few bars
and restaurants are
available at Camacha.

Tornos and Curral dos Romeiros. At a signposted path junction, stop and make a decision. For a bit of adventure, then turn left uphill. If you suffer from vertigo or prefer an easier path, then turn right downhill. Both routes meet again at Curral dos Romeiros.

The path to the left, signposted for the Levada dos Tornos, is broad and clear, climbing beside a steep rocky cutting. Pass eucalyptus and mimosa, followed by pines. The Levada dos Tornos is reached where it emerges from a tunnel. Follow the water downstream from the tunnel mouth and pass a stone arch. The levada has a narrow parapet and some stretches are exposed. Take care, as there is no protection where the cliff falls precipitously, though there is often a screen of trees and shrubs. There are views across the valley to Babosas, and down to the harbour at Funchal. At **Curral dos Romeiros**, houses cling to a steep slope. The levada is covered, and when it flows beneath a house, walk down steps and turn left to walk along a cobbled track. Watch for a sign on the left for the Levada dos Tornos and Camacha, where steps lead back up to the levada.

The easier alternative zig-zags down from the junction, and the track passes tall eucalyptus. Street lights accompany the track across a bridge over a bouldery riverbed. Follow the track up a slope covered in laurel and mimosa. There is a signposted junction where zig-zags lead up to the left for **Curral dos Romeiros**, passing tall eucalyptus. Simply follow the most obvious track straight through the village, walking on concrete or cobbles. Avoid turnings to right and left, until almost landing on a road near a bus stop. Watch for a sign on the left for the Levada dos Tornos and Camacha, where steps lead back up to the levada.

After leaving Curral dos Romeiros, the next valley has dense laurel cover. Mimosa and eucalyptus appear later, while agapanthus and brambles flank the path. After looping round small valleys, the levada is crossed by flights of steps and the next few houses are at **Choupana**. Cross a narrow road and go through a gateway in a tall wall. A fence runs close to the levada and leaves little room to manoeuvre past a house. Pass a water intake and

Agapanthus and eucalyptus grow alongside the Levada dos Tornos

cross a steep road. Continue past eucalyptus and a small farm, then make tight turns to cross a couple of streams. After a wooded stretch, walk through a concrete tunnel beneath a road. There are bus services if required. A battered road is reached near the delightful Hortensia Gardens **Tea House**. Follow the levada further and enjoy views of Funchal and the Ilhas Desertas. Walk through woods and cross a road at a bend. Eucalyptus and pines flank the levada, then there is a break in the tree cover near the Jasmin Tea House. Walk onwards into a quiet wooded valley. Pass a pink house with apples alongside. The levada reaches the busy ER-102 road, so cross carefully on a bend at Lombo da Quinta.

Pass a water intake and keep left of the Technialia building. Cross a road and turn left to continue along the levada, but note the **Bar** Maio nearby offering refreshments. Apples give way to dense eucalyptus and mimosa. Reach a **tunnel** entrance, then either go through the tunnel or follow a path over it. Going through requires a torch, as the path is narrow and there is low headroom. Continue through woods to a road called the Rua do Pomar and turn right. The levada drifts away to the left and is less wooded. Chestnut and oak are seen while swinging round the valley, and there is a knot of bamboo at the valley head. Note the steps to the left, where a sign promises ice cream! As the levada passes houses at **Nogueira**, the channel is covered in concrete. Do not follow it beyond the village, as there is a rather messy tunnel. Follow the road uphill instead, passing the Pastelaria Candeeiro snack bar.

Walk straight up the road through a housing estate, avoiding turnings to right and left. There are bus stops if an early finish is needed, otherwise walk to a road junction facing the large Laboratório Agrícola de Madeira. Turn left up the ER-205 road, then right along the Travessa João Claudio Nobrega. Follow the road beside the laboratory, then keep straight on downhill at a junction. The road winds down through **Ribeirinha**, passing a number of houses, pines and eucalyptus trees. Follow the road uphill, and for future reference, note a sign on the right marking the continuation of the Levada dos Tornos. Cross a wooded rise, then turn left up the Caminho Fonte Concelos. The road swings left and climbs in the shade of tall trees. To enter the village of **Camacha**, turn right to climb past a modern church and reach a square. There are plenty of places offering food and drink, as well as shady places where you can relax. There are toilets on the square and the bus stop is just across the road. A monument declares that the first game of football ever played in Portugal was completed here in 1875. Just to one side of the square is a basket factory, which is well worth a visit and features traditional and modern designs.

Walk 2: Levada dos Tornos – part 2

THE ROUTE

Distance:
18km (11 miles).

Start:
In the middle of Camacha – 273170.

Finish:
At Quatro Estradas on the ER-102 road – 288204.

Maps:
Military Survey 1:25,000 Sheets 6 and 9
or IGC 1:50,000 Madeira East.

Terrain:
There are a few short tunnels. The levada path may be wet, slippery or exposed for short stretches. The slopes are wooded and cultivated.

Leave the square in the middle of Camacha and walk downhill by road past the modern church. Turn left down a road called the Caminho Fonte Concelos, which runs past tall trees. Keep right at a couple of road junctions and another road crosses a rise to descend to **Ribeirinha**. Watch carefully on the left to spot a sign for the Levada dos Tornos. Pick a way along a terrace to reach a slope of tall pines and follow a narrow path downhill. On reaching the Levada dos Tornos, cross over and turn left. Cross a steep road, then there is another steep road at some houses. Continue through woods and along a concrete path to reach more houses and a tunnel. The **tunnel** is short and the water from the levada flows through a pipeline. The path is good, but the roof is a bit low.

Emerge from the tunnel and follow the pipeline past a couple of houses on the side of a wide valley. There are views, but it is also fairly well wooded in places. Cross a footbridge and follow the pipeline through another

The walkable length of the Levada dos Tornos is about 27km (16¼ miles), but by the time extra distance is added to join and leave the watercourse, it is a little longer. This stretch from Camacha to Quatro Estradas is about 16km (10 miles), but includes a bit extra at the start and finish. There are a few short tunnels on the first part of this walk, and a torch is useful, though not absolutely necessary. There are some short, steep, rocky stretches too, where the path can be narrow and slippery. The route alternates between wooded slopes and cultivated terraces, and the general altitude of the levada is just below 600m (1970ft).

35

Transport:
Camacha Bus 29, 77 and
110 serve Camacha.
Camacha Bus 113 serves
Lombo Grande.
Camacha Bus 77 serves
Quatro Estradas. Taxis at
Camacha.

Refreshments:
There are a few bars and
restaurants at the start in
Camacha.

tunnel. There is good headroom this time, though the path can be wet. Follow the pipeline onwards, and take care not to trip over concrete supports, which jut across the path. It may be wet and slippery as the path narrows at the head of the valley. Climb up and down steps to pass a water intake building, then cross a levada stepping stone footbridge over the **Ribeira do Porto Novo**.

Pass a weeping wall and turn round a densely wooded spur into a little side valley. Watch out for rock overhanging the path. Turn round the little valley, then walk through chestnut and pines. Go under a little bridge to reach another short **tunnel**. There is a good path and good headroom, then a brambly corner. At another **tunnel** a torch might be useful as it is curved. The path is mostly good and there is good headroom. There are some short, exposed stretches further along, as well as views across the valley to Camacha. Pass a mixture of trees and shrubs, before crossing a steep and narrow road.

Follow a concrete path with street lights alongside and cross another steep and narrow road. Agapanthus and tall pines grow alongside the levada, then pass a water intake and small reservoir. The path is broad as it turns round **Lombo Grande**, leading to a road where there are bus stops. There is a view from the road bend to the jagged Ponta de São Lourenço. Cross the road to continue walking into denser woods, with a mixture of trees and shrubs alongside. Cross a narrow road where there are a few buildings.

The levada runs past pines to reach the head of a little valley where there are also chestnuts and willows. The valley is mostly cultivated then, on leaving, cross a steep concrete track. Turn into the next little valley, which is also cultivated, and go through a short tunnel. The path is uneven and headroom is limited. Follow the levada onwards, passing a house and stands of pine and eucalyptus. There are a few chestnuts, and some of the pines later have charred trunks. Enter another little valley where the vegetation is tangled and willow grows at the head. After turning round a tiny valley with a few houses and terraces at **Eiras Velhas**, masses of agapanthus grow beside the levada, then a derelict house is passed.

Looking down on old farmhouses at the end of the Levada dos Tornos

The path narrows and drops below the levada for a short while and the view down the valley reveals the Ilhas Desertas out to sea. Take care on a narrow concrete parapet along a rocky edge. Make your way into a steep-walled, well-wooded gorge, and cross a levada stepping stone footbridge over the Ribeiro dos Vinháticos. There is another rocky edge to negotiate. Turn into a side valley and admire the cultivation terraces in the main valley. Willows grow at the head of the side valley, then there are pines and eucalyptus. The path becomes concrete and has street lights, leading past apples and houses to cross a cobbled road at **Ribeira do Eixo**.

Follow the levada past nurseries, where there are loops across a slope where trees have been felled and replanted. After walking past taller trees, pass a circular reservoir and cross a road. After a short way, cross another road and turn round a blunt nose on a hillside where there are tall pines, mimosa and eucalyptus. Some of the mimosa is quite tall on the way round another little valley. Leave the valley and turn a corner, with a view down to the airport and the Ilhas Desertas beyond. Walk past many pines and chestnuts before gaining another view, then there is more mimosa and tall eucalyptus, with agapanthus alongside. There is a bit of a rocky stretch before another turn, then willow grows around the head of the next little valley. Mixed woodlands include laurels on leaving the valley, then cross a steep tarmac road and pass a house.

Head into the next little valley, where there are views between the trees to small farm buildings. The head of the valley is a jungle, but there are later views down the main valley, drained by the **Ribeira de Santa Cruz.** You could walk to the end of the Levada dos Tornos by passing a sloping metal pipe crossing the levada. To finish the walk, however, turn left up a flight of cobbled steps beforehand. A path leads to a couple of houses, where a left turn leads up a cobbled road. Climb steeply at first, then more gently through a crossroads. A tarmac road, called the Estrada Municipal Mary Jane Wilson, leads straight uphill out of the trees to reach a crossroads at Quatro Estradas. There are bus stops either side of the junction.

WALK 3: *Levada da Serra – part 1*

THE ROUTE
Distance:
11km (7 miles).
Start:
On the ER-201 road above São João de Latrão –
242157.
Finish:
In the middle of Camacha – 273170.
Maps:
Military Survey 1:25,000 Sheet 9 or IGC 1:50,000
Madeira East.
Terrain:
The levada path is generally clear, easy to follow and
almost level. The surroundings are generally well
wooded with some cultivated areas.

There is no bus giving direct access to the start of the
Levada da Serra, so use Funchal Bus 47 to reach a point
high on the ER-201 road above São João de Latrão. When
the bus turns downhill, continue walking along the bendy
high road to pass the **Campo do Pomar** sports ground. At
a crossroads, the cobbled road called the Caminho do
Pico do Infante rises to the right. It is signposted for the
Levada da Serra do Faial, to use the full title. There is a
bendy stretch on the ascent, then turn right as signposted.

There is no water in the narrow cut alongside the
path. The slopes are covered in eucalyptus, chestnut,
laurel and pine. Follow the path onwards and it is mostly
eucalyptus growing, which colonised the slope after a
fire. A few charred chestnuts survived the blaze. The
ground cover is bracken and brambles, with agapanthus
growing beside the path. There are glimpses of Funchal,
then a ruined stone building is passed. Walk round a
valley above Lombo da Quinta and there are a few habitations below the levada. There is more evidence of the

It is possible to walk
the whole of the
Levada da Serra in a
day. It measures about
25km (15½ miles), but
the climb up to it and
descent from it
increases the walking
distance. It is better to
split the route into
unequal halves and
break at Camacha. This
first stretch covers the
ascent from São João, a
walk along the levada,
and the descent to
Camacha. The levada is
usually dry at first, but
there is more water as
the walk progresses
gently upstream. The
route is well wooded
with a variety of tall
trees, and there is often
a margin of
agapanthus. At the
beginning of the walk
the levada is at an
altitude of 760m
(2495ft), rising to 800m
(2625ft) above
Camacha.

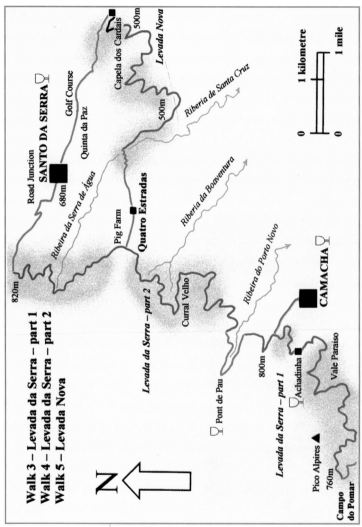

Walk 3 – Levada da Serra – part 1
Walk 4 – Levada da Serra – part 2
Walk 5 – Levada Nova

fire that devastated the woods, but there has been some replanting in an enclosure. After that point, notice what the slopes were like before the fire, passing well-established chestnut, oak, mimosa and laurel. There may be water in the levada, now followed faithfully upstream. Leaving the valley, cross a gentle rise over a short tunnel, crossing a track at the same time.

Walk through dense woodlands and cross a bridge over the bouldery Ribeiro da Abegoaria. Swing round a bend where there are tall pines, oaks and laurels, all covered in climbing ivy. Cross a track with a blocked gateway, then cross a track leading up to the **Quinta de Vale Paraiso.** The grand old house is used as a children's home. Views from this point take in the Ilhas Desertas. The main road below is noisy, while the track beside the levada runs though lovely mature woodlands. Cross a road near a house called Casa do Reviver.

Transport: Funchal Bus 47 to reach the start. Camacha Bus 111 serves Achadinha. Camacha Bus 29, 77 and 110 serve Camacha.

Refreshments: The Snack Bar Moisés is at Achadinha and there are a few bars and restaurants at the end in Camacha.

A few houses above Lombo da Quinta on the Levada da Serra.

41

The levada continues and the path is flanked by trees, with a few houses above and below. Swing round across a stream, then later cross a steep and patchy road. A house called Quinta Proteas is just uphill. Continue along the wooded path, noting the pines growing in the valley, though there are other well-established trees, including oaks with scorched trunks. The higher parts of the valley are under rampant bracken and gorse. Pass well below a tall fence, later passing close to a massive concrete buttress that holds a sports ground in place. The path is pleasantly wooded, with views between the trees, then cross a narrow road called the Caminho da Madeira.

A slope covered in pines gives way to denser woods, then later the path drops down a flight of steps onto a road at **Achadinha**, where there are bus stops. Turn left and walk a short way up to a crossroads, where a break can be taken at the Snack Bar Moisés.

Walk straight through the crossroads past the Snack Bar Moisés, as signposted for the Levada da Serra – Faial. A concrete road passes a few houses, with the levada to the left. A rugged track and clear path lead into lovely mixed woods, and there are street lights alongside while traversing the valley sides. A track leads past houses and reaches a crossroads with the Caminho Municipal da Portela. Either continue along the levada by referring to Walk 4, or turn right and follow the road down to Camacha.

On reaching **Camacha**, walk down to a square in the middle of the village. There are plenty of places offering food and drink, as well as shady places where you can relax. There are toilets on the square and the bus stop is just across the road. A monument declares that the first game of football ever played in Portugal was completed here in 1875. Just to one side of the square is a basket factory, which is well worth a visit and features traditional and modern designs.

WALK 4: Levada da Serra – part 2

THE ROUTE
Distance:
21km (13 miles).
Start:
In the middle of Camacha – 273170.
Finish:
In the middle of Santo da Serra – 298218.
Maps:
Military Survey 1:25,000 Sheets 6 and 9 or IGC
1:50,000 Madeira East.
Terrain:
The levada path is generally clear, easy to follow and
almost level. The surroundings are generally well
wooded with some cultivated areas.

Leave **Camacha** by walking up the road signposted for
Santo da Serra. Turn left at the Super Mercado Vila da
Camacha and follow the quieter Caminho Municipal da
Portela uphill. Turn right at a crossroads to follow the
Levada da Serra. The track is wooded, with street lights
alongside, crossing a stream and traversing the other side
of a valley, where there are more houses. The track leads
onwards, then the levada suddenly ducks into a tunnel
on the left. The track runs up to a road, which is followed
only a few paces downhill before turning left at a junction. Walk down the road a short way to see the tunnel
again on the left. The road has been constructed along
the course of the Levada da Serra, which is now buried
beneath, so follow the road around the valley.

Eucalyptus and oak grow beside the road, though
later there is more terracing and cultivation, with plenty
of houses stacked on the sunny slopes. The road eventually swings round to the right and crosses a bridge over
the **Ribeira do Porto Novo**. Take a break at the Snack Bar

The Levada da Serra
measures about 25km
(15½ miles), and breaks
into two unequal
halves that are more
easily walked. The
longer stretch is from
Camacha to Santo da
Serra. Start by climbing
above Camacha to link
with the levada, then
follow it gradually
upstream. In one valley,
the levada lies beneath
a road, but for the most
part it wanders round
quiet valleys, often well
wooded, with a few
open stretches. At the
end, either continue
along the Levada da
Portela or follow a
track and roads down
to Santo da Serra. The
levada is at an altitude
of 800m (2625ft) above
Camacha, rising to
820m (2690ft) above
Santo da Serra.

Transport:
Camacha Bus 29, 77 and
110 serve Camacha.
Camacha Bus 77 and
SAM Bus 20 serve Santo
da Serra.

Refreshments:
There are bars and
restaurants at Camacha
and Santo da Serra. The
only place between them
is the Snack Bar Pont de
Pau.

Pont de Pau, or keep walking along the road. Pass through a cutting surmounted by a small bridge, then make loops into a couple of side valleys. When the road begins to run downhill, turn left along another road. It is a short road leading onto a track, and the levada is on the left again.

The track cuts across a slope of pines and eucalyptus, though a line of oaks march alongside the levada. Enter a pleasant little valley and cross a concrete road. The line of oaks becomes a trademark for the levada, while the slopes alongside carry plenty of broom. There is another wooded stretch, as well as a bare area where there was a landslip. The levada makes a pronounced left bend in the trees and crosses a new road. Keep following the clear path alongside. Passing above **Curral Velho**, there is a stone-crushing plant down in the valley, then the levada aims for the quieter head of the wooded valley. There are oaks beside the track, as well as broom and tree heather. Cross a stout bridge over the Ribeiro dos Vinháticos, and walk on top of a massive stone buttress. There are denser woodlands around a derelict building. Pass above the stone-crushing plant again, and notice the vigorous growths of hydrangeas beside the levada. Views down the valley frame the Ilhas Desertas out to sea, while in the next valley it is suddenly very quiet and richly wooded.

Walk through a short tunnel and continue along the levada. Cross a bridge in the next valley and note how the water is drawn off along a lower levada. Keep following the track to pass through a couple of cuttings, with no water in sight. The area is covered in straggly eucalyptus, then reach a road beside a large **pig farm**. (For a quick exit from the walk, follow the road down to the crossroads at Quatro Estradas to catch a bus.)

A sign points back along the levada to Camacha, and ahead to Portela. Follow a clear track alongside the piggery fence, then exchange pig odour for more pleasing eucalyptus scent. The trademark line of oaks still march beside the levada, as well as hydrangeas. There are fine views across the eastern parts of Madeira, with laurels and pleasant loops further along. Eucalyptus trees have

been felled near the **Ribeira da Serra de Agua**, then there are denser stands of laurel and tree heather, some of them hoary with lichens. The levada makes a series of loops through rampant vegetation, then reaches a broad and clear track. The levada cuts across the track, and could be followed either to Portela or Ribeiro Frio by referring to Walk 6 or Walk 7.

To finish at Santo da Serra, turn right and follow the track down through wonderfully mixed woods. There is a large house to the left on leaving the woods, then the access road swings left and right to drop down to the main ER-102 road. Turn right and follow the road carefully round a right-hand bend. There are bus stops if you want to finish the walk fairly quickly, otherwise turn left along the ER-212 as signposted for **Santo da Serra**. The road leads into the village, where food and drink can be obtained while waiting for a bus.

WALK 5: Levada Nova – Santo da Serra

THE ROUTE

Distance:

13km (8 miles).

Start:

At Quatro Estradas on the ER-102 road – 288204.

Finish:

In the middle of Santo da Serra – 298218.

Maps:

Military Survey 1:25,000 Sheet 6 or IGC 1:50,000 Madeira East.

Terrain:

The descent to the Ribeira de Santa Cruz can be steep and difficult, but the Levada Nova generally has a good and easy path. The ascent to Santo da Serra at the end is along roads.

Start at **Quatro Estradas** on the ER-102 road between Camacha and Santo da Serra. Follow the road downhill, which is the Estrada Municipal Mary Jane Wilson, passing mimosa, eucalyptus and pine. After passing a junction with another narrow road, head off to the left down a narrow cobbled road, passing tall pine and cedar. Walk more gently down through a crossroads, then more steeply down to a couple of houses in a small cultivated area. Turn right down a stony path alongside a field, then stony zig-zag steps lead down to the Levada dos Tornos. Turn left along the levada, but look carefully to spot a path descending to the right. This path is worn and awkward in places, but it leads to a concrete bridge over the **Ribeira de Santa Cruz**. A path and steps lead a short way up a well-wooded slope to the **Levada Nova**.

Turn left to see how water is drawn from the river to feed the levada. Turn right, however, to start making headway downstream. The valley is wonderfully wild and wooded, but also wet in places, and the path may be slippery where it narrows. There is a rocky stretch and a view of a little waterfall below, then the levada crosses a cultivated slope. After picking a walk along another rocky edge, agapanthus flanks the path and the tree cover is mostly tall eucalyptus. Cross a steep concrete road.

A broad earth path is flanked by agapanthus and mimosa as the levada curves round a small valley. Cross a levada stepping-stone footbridge in tall mixed woodlands and walk to another steep concrete road. There is a water intake on one side of the road and a house on the other. Pass the house and swing round into the next big valley, with a good view across the valley, though eucalyptus blocks views while turning round a little side valley. Agapanthus and brambles flank the path on leaving the little valley, with mimosa below and the remains of tall pines on the slope above. Turn round the slope and enter another valley, crossing another levada stepping-stone footbridge. Mimosa and eucalyptus flourish on leaving the valley, then towards the head of the main valley, cross an exposed rocky slope for a short way. A levada stepping-stone footbridge spans the Ribeira do Moreno.

There is another short, exposed, rocky stretch while leaving the valley, and there is also quite a tangle of eucalyptus in a little side valley. Leave the little valley and turn round a slope covered in burnt tree trunks. There is plenty of bracken cover, with mimosa and eucalyptus growing too. Enter another little side valley full of eucalyptus and cross yet another levada stepping-stone footbridge. Pass a big white house on leaving the valley and there is a view back across the main valley.

Cross a track and walk through mimosa, then agapanthus and brambles flank the path. Cross a concrete road between a lumberyard and piggery, then later cross a tarmac road. The levada runs between tall fences as it passes a building, then it enters another little valley. Eucalyptus grows at the head of the valley and another levada stepping-stone footbridge is crossed. Mimosa grows as the levada leaves the valley, and in places the path is flanked with long grass, bracken and brambles. Walk around a bigger valley, where mixed woodlands give way to pine cover, which in turn gives way to more mimosa and eucalyptus. The levada makes a couple of tight turns, then suddenly flows more noticeably down to reach a storage tank beside a little white chapel. This is the **Capela dos Cardais** and there is a car park alongside.

The Levada Nova offers a pleasant walk on wooded and cultivated slopes high above Santa Cruz and the airport. Bus services do not really go near it, but you can start from Quatro Estradas between Camacha and Santo da Serra and link with the levada. This involves walking down to the Ribeira de Santa Cruz, from where the levada initially draws its water. Follow the levada gently downstream to finish at the Capela dos Cardais. Either walk steeply downhill to finish at Água de Pena, or walk less steeply uphill to finish at Santo da Serra.

Transport:
Camacha Bus 77 serves
Quatro Estradas.
Camacha Bus 77 and
SAM Bus 20 serve Santo
da Serra.

Refreshments:
There are bars and
restaurants at the end in
Santo da Serra.

*A little waterfall in the
valley near the start of
the Levada Nova*

If you can arrange to be met here by someone with a car,
then you can omit the final road walk.

Turn left to follow the road uphill, with trees alongside. Pass the lower part of the Santo da Serra **Golf Course**
and reach a road junction. Turn right as signposted for
Santo da Serra. The road rises alongside the golf course
and there are views eastwards to the rugged Ponta de São
Lourenço and west to Pico do Areeiro. Pass a road junction at the gateway of **Quinta da Paz** and continue along
a more wooded part of the road to reach **Santo da Serra**.
Bars and restaurants offer food and drink while waiting
for a bus.

WALK 6: *Levada da Portela*

THE ROUTE
Distance:
8km (5 miles).
Start:
Junction of the ER-102 and ER-212 near Santo da Serra – 291221.
Finish:
On the gap at Portela – 293244.
Maps:
Military Survey 1:25,000 Sheet 6 or IGC 1:50,000 Madeira East.
Terrain:
Paths and tracks are generally easy and clear. The higher parts are well wooded. Some steep paths on the descent can be slippery when wet.

Enjoy a walk along the Levada da Portela by starting on the main road between Camacha and Portela, climbing up to the levada, then following it across the slope and down to Portela. The slopes are well wooded and the route is quite interesting, as well as being short and easily accomplished. While the higher parts of the levada are generally level, the water makes a rather abrupt descent, reaching Portela more quickly than the fastest walker. The higher parts of the levada are at 830m (2725ft), while Portela sits on a gap at 670m (2200ft).

Transport:
Camacha Bus 77 and SAM Bus 20 and 78 serve Santo da Serra. SAM Bus 53, 56 and 78 serve Portela.

Refreshments:
There are a couple of restaurants at Portela at the end.

This walk could be started at Santo da Serra, but the initial road-walk can be limited by starting at the **road junction** of the ER-102 and ER-212 roads near the village. Follow the road as signposted for Portela, turning carefully round a left-hand bend. On the left is a quiet road rising uphill, and some of the SAM Bus services pass this junction. Follow the quiet road round a sharp bend, then pass a large house and continue along a broad and clear track into mixed woodland. The track begins to bend as it climbs. Look out for a levada on the right, then follow it a short way to reach a flat grassy area at a water tower. There are route directions painted on the side of the tower, including indicators for Portela and Ribeiro Frio. This is a popular place for walkers to take a break, with curiously contorted cedars alongside.

A line of tall cedars and dense laurels line the Levada da Portela further along. The parapet beside the levada is very narrow as the channel picks its way across a rocky

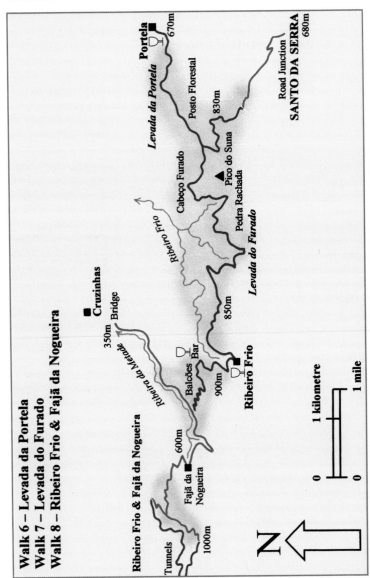

Walk 6 – Levada da Portela
Walk 7 – Levada do Furado
Walk 8 – Ribeiro Frio & Fajã da Nogueira

Portela 670m

Levada da Portela

Posto Florestal

830m

SANTO DA SERRA 680m

Road Junction

Pico do Suna

Cabeço Furado

Pedra Rachada

Ribeiro Frio

Levada do Furado

850m

Cruzinhas

Bridge

350m

Ribeira da Metade

Balcões

900m

Bar

Ribeiro Frio

600m

Fajã da Nogueira

1000m

Tunnels

Ribeiro Frio & Fajã da Nogueira

1 kilometre
1 mile

0   0

N

50

outcrop. Do not follow the levada, but use a path that
runs below it for a while. The path leading onwards is
broad and clear, again flanked by tall cedars. There is a
very pronounced bend to the left at a small tunnel, then
the levada describes little curves as it crosses the wooded
slope. Emerge in the open on a broad track, where signposts point back to Camacha and Santo da Serra, as well
as ahead for Ribeiro Frio. Either follow the track downhill in the direction of Portela, or follow the levada a little
further. If the levada is followed, then switch to the right
at a path junction. The surroundings remain well wooded,
and the path quickly reaches a signposted junction near
another water tower.

Walk carefully down a flight of slippery steps from
the water tower, then follow the narrow water-chute,
which is the **Levada da Portela**. The water races downhill
and quickly leads to a broad dirt road at the **Posto
Florestal**. There are toilets and a picnic garden at this
point. Follow the dirt road downhill, passing another
picnic viewpoint on the way. Continue down as signposted for Portela. Look out for a track on the left that
leads to a gateway, then continue straight along a grassy
track to pass Lombo das Faias. The path is flanked by a
tangle of bracken, brambles and gorse, but listen to hear
the water rushing along the levada. The water cuts
beneath the path and flows down a wooded slope. Later,
go down a flight of steps flanked by hydrangeas and
agapanthus. The path leads into a stand of mimosa and
also passes tall cedars, then crude steps lead down to the
ER-102 road. Turn left to walk down the road to the gap
at **Portela**. There is a roadside viewpoint looking towards
Penha de Águia. There may be taxis parked nearby,
though there are buses too. For food and drink, head for
the Restaurante Miradouro da Portela or the Restaurante
Portela à Vista.

*Water rushing through
the narrow channel of
the Levada da Portela*

WALK 7: Levada do Furado

The Levada do Furado was cut from a very steep slope covered in ancient 'laurisilva' woodland. Enjoy the splendidly rugged course it takes around the mountainside, but be warned that there are exposed cliffs, even though the woods mask the exposure. The levada passes through a series of short tunnels, and some wet stretches can be slippery underfoot. The aim is to reach the road at Ribeiro Frio, where there is a restaurant and a bar. Note that maps show the line of the levada wrongly; the watercourse is actually aligned to the 850m (2790ft) contour.

THE ROUTE
Distance:
11km (6³/₄ miles).
Start:
On the gap at Portela – 293244.
Finish:
At the Restaurante Ribeiro Frio – 36231.
Maps:
Military Survey 1:25,000 Sheet 6 or IGC 1:50,000 Madeira East.
Terrain:
Paths, tracks and steps are used on the ascent from Portela. The Levada do Furado is exposed, rocky and slippery in places, and nearly always well wooded. The path towards the end is clear, level and easy.

Start on the gap at **Portela** at 670m (2200ft). For food or drink at the start, visit the Restaurante Miradouro da Portela or Restaurante Portela à Vista. Follow the ER-102 road uphill in the direction of Santa da Serra. Turn right up a path and climb a flight of crude steps alongside the Levada da Portela. Pass tall cedars, then emerge from a stand of mimosa to find a flight of steps flanked by hydrangeas and agapanthus. After climbing up the steps, continue to follow the path up a wooded slope. At a higher level, the levada suddenly switches from the left to the right of the path. There is a tangle of bracken, brambles and gorse alongside. A grassy track leads past a gateway at Lombo das Faias, and a clearer track leads onwards. Turn right up a broad and clear dirt road, climbing up past a picnic viewpoint to reach the **Posto Florestal**. There are toilets and a picnic garden here. Pass the house and take a path to the right, which climbs further uphill. The levada is in a narrow water-chute. Climb a flight of slippery steps to reach a water tower at a junction with the levadas. Turn right to start following the levada towards Ribeiro Frio.

The channel slices through mossy rock, and runs through dense laurel and tree heather. Trees obscure the fact that the levada clings to a very steep and rocky slope. Marvel at the engineering of the watercourse while following it upstream. There is a series of small tunnels; some of them for walking through and others for walking past. Sometimes there are views between the trees, and though the levada path may be narrow and exposed at times, there is some fencing alongside. Sometimes the cutting in the rock overhangs the channel, and the path along the parapet is narrow, while at other times there is enough space on the slope to accommodate quite a broad path. The last of the short tunnels is more like a narrow rocky chasm at **Cabeço Furado**.

The path is broad and well wooded for a while, then becomes uneven. There is a pronounced rocky left turn into the valley of **Pedra Rachada**, where there are well-established laurels and tree heather. The path is broad and easy in places, but sometimes rough, rocky, narrow and exposed. Watch for the path dipping below the levada where the channel has been cut across a green and slippery weeping wall. Watch for a couple more of these little by-pass routes, then there is a good stretch without any real difficulties before reaching another weeping wall where the path dips again. After an easy stretch the levada runs though a couple of short tunnels and rocky notches.

The levada noses into a couple of damp, mossy, fern-clad valleys. Turning round both valleys, the path dips below the level of the levada to avoid narrow and slippery parapets. There is an interesting green pool in the second valley. The path is quite narrow as it curves around the Lombo do Capitão, but it becomes easy and well wooded. Cross a bridge over the Ribeira do Poço do Bezerro. The path is broad and well wooded as it leaves the valley and there is a pronounced swing into the next valley. The path narrows and there is a fence alongside, but it is not too exposed. After passing another weeping wall, swing round a rocky corner at Cabeço do

Transport:
SAM Bus 53, 56 and 78 serve Portela. São Roque Bus 56, 103 and 138 serve Ribeiro Frio.

Refreshments:
There are a couple of bars and restaurants at Portela and Ribeiro Frio.

Pessegueiro. The levada runs through a small tunnel and there is a bigger cave off to the left.

Traffic can be heard on the road across the densely wooded valley, and a building is seen in the woods, so despite the tree cover, Ribeiro Frio is nearby. The path is rough and rocky, passing through a rocky notch. After another rugged stretch, things get easier and hydrangeas grow alongside the path, which seem alien after walking so long through the 'laurisilva'. Note an old mill over the river, then cross a bridge. There is an information board explaining about the nature of the 'laurisilva' woods and the wealth of flowers and birdlife that it supports. A flight of steps leads up to the ER-103 road at **Ribeiro Frio**. The Restaurante Ribeiro Frio is immediately to hand and there is a bar and the Cold River Souvenirs shop across the road.

WALK 8: Ribeiro Frio and Fajã da Nogueira

THE ROUTE
Distance:
16km (10 miles).
Start:
At the Restaurante Ribeiro Frio – 236231.
Finish:
Bridge over the Ribeira da Metade below Cruzinhas – 242252.
Maps:
Military Survey 1:25,000 Sheet 6 or IGC 1:50,000 Madeira East.
Terrain:
Some broad and clear tracks, but also steep and narrow paths. There are plenty of steep, wooded slopes. A narrow and exposed levada walk includes ten small tunnels.

Although Fajã da Nogueira can be reached by following a dirt road up the Metade valley, it is more interesting to approach it from Ribeiro Frio and Balcões. An easy levada walk from Ribeiro Frio leads to a fine viewpoint at Balcões that allows the layout of the valley to be studied, overlooking the generating station at Fajã da Nogueira and the peaks that tower above it. A zig-zag path leads down a steep, wooded slope into the valley, then on reaching the generating station, a track leads up to the Levada da Serra. This watercourse offers an exciting and exposed walk round the head of the valley.

Start at the Restaurante **Ribeiro Frio** and walk a short way down the road and round a corner. A signpost for Balcões stands beside a notice giving details of the birdlife that can be spotted in the 'laurisilva' woodlands. The levada channel is narrow, but the path alongside is broad. Walk through mixed woods and enter a little valley to cross a concrete bridge. Leaving the valley, the levada is covered as it runs a short way through a rock cutting. Wind across the slope, pass a house selling drinks and souvenirs, then pass above the **Balcões Bar**. There is another rock cutting, then the broad path crosses a well-wooded slope and goes through yet another little cutting. A paved path leads off to the right to the Miradouro dos **Balcões**. There is a rocky tor and a fine viewpoint, looking down the Metade valley to Penha de Águia and up the valley to Pico do Areeiro, Pico do Gato, Torres, Pico Ruivo and Achada do

Transport:
São Roque Bus 56,103
and 110 serve Ribeiro
Frio and Cruzinhas.

Refreshments:
There are a couple of
bars and restaurants at
Ribeiro Frio.

Teixeira. There is also a clear view of the generating station at Fajã da Nogueira.

Double back up the path and turn right to follow the levada further. The path narrows and two black plastic pipes carry water through the levada channel. The channel is covered in slabs across a short rockface, then it is narrow and uneven, mossy in places and slippery when wet. Look out for a path down to the right, and do not be tempted to follow the levada further, as it is in a very bad state of repair. The path descends and has some crude stone steps, then it rises a little. Continue downhill and pass below two enormous mossy boulders, then cross a more open slope of heather. Back in the woods, continue down a zig-zag path that is quite steep and vague at times. At the bottom of the wooded slope, cross a bouldery stream and follow it a short way, then step up onto a broad dirt road.

Turn left to follow the road up the valley towards Fajã da Nogueira. There is a striking view of Torres, before the road swings left to pass a building and a tunnel mouth. Water flowing into this tunnel emerges as the Levada dos Tornos (see Walk 1 and Walk 2). Cross a bridge over a bouldery river, then follow the road up to the generating station at **Fajã da Nogueira**. The peaks of Torres and Pico do Gato are seen while turning a bend below the buildings. Approach some houses, but turn right up a stony track beforehand. The track rises in easy loops on a well-wooded slope. A sign points out that two big til trees alongside the track are the oldest discovered on the island, asking you to respect them. Turn right at a junction of tracks and keep climbing past more big, old tils. The track leads to the Levada da Serra, which is covered in slabs in both directions. By all means turn right and enjoy the view down the Metade valley, but this route turns left to explore the head of the valley.

After walking along the slabbed-over section, There is an open stretch of the levada running downstream. The path is wide at first, then passes through two little **tunnels**, turns round an exposed gully, and goes through another little tunnel. There is a curious bendy tunnel next, then the parapet is fenced and unfenced across a cliff face.

A covered stretch of the Levada da Serra above Fajã da Nogueira

Go through a short and low tunnel, which has a 'window' part way along. The channel is covered where the path is uneven across an open slope. Go through another bendy tunnel, which has a low entrance and exit, with a couple of 'windows' along its length. The levada is quite bendy afterwards. Walk along the parapet, then walk beside it. There is no need to enter the next tunnel, as there is a rugged path below the rock-face. Plenty of tree heather grows on the slopes and a fenced path runs below the parapet. Enter the next bendy tunnel, which has a double arch at its exit. Step up onto the parapet, then step down

57

to enter yet another bendy tunnel. This one is quite low, featuring another 'window'. The parapet leads round a rocky gully that is unfenced and exposed, then there are short lengths of fencing. Walk on and off the parapet as required, passing some big tils and noticing Pico do Gato at the head of the valley. Cross a bouldery gully and pass a tin hut, then turn round an exposed corner. It is mostly fenced afterwards, then the path continues beside the parapet and crosses a stone arched bridge over the bouldery river at the head of the valley.

Walk along or beside the parapet as required, with or without fencing alongside. There is a curve round an undercut, dripping cliff where the levada is unfenced, but covered by slabs. Go through a little tunnel, then it is mostly fenced afterwards. Slabs cover a stretch and there are good views down the valley. Go through a small cutting and round another curved, dripping cliff, noting a side-feed from a tunnel. Go through a short, tall tunnel and continue walking on and off the parapet, where the path is fenced and unfenced, until the next tunnel. Do not enter this one, but go down stone steps to the left, then down crude wooden steps, zig-zagging downhill among tall tils. Turn right at a track junction and walk down to the river. Either ford the flow or cross a rickety footbridge. The track drifts away from the river, climbing with less woodland alongside, to reach a junction of tracks passed earlier in the walk. Turn right to walk back down to the generating station.

Follow the dirt road down through the valley, first by retracing steps across the bridge over the bouldery river, passing the tunnel mouth and building. Pass the stream where the road was first joined earlier in the day, and continue gently down through the valley. There are hardly any buildings, but there are some cultivated areas along the way. Reach the main ER-103 road at a bridge over the **Ribeira da Metade** below Cruzinhas. If there is any length of time to wait for a bus, it is a long walk to a bar!

WALK 9: North Coast Walk

THE ROUTE

Distance:
12km (71/2 miles).

Start:
At the church in Porto da Cruz – 292272.

Finish:
At the Bar Boca do Risco at Ribeira Seca – 342227.

Maps:
Military Survey 1:25,000 Sheet 6 or
IGC 1:50,000 Madeira East.

Terrain:
Roads and tracks lead uphill, then a well-wooded path
cuts across a slope. Later, the slope is more open and
exposed in places, becoming wooded again afterwards.
An easy valley path leads downhill at the end.

There is a splendid cliff coast path heading eastwards from Porto da Cruz on the north coast of Madeira. Follow a winding road uphill to reach it, then although the first stages are well wooded, later parts are quite open and feature dramatic scenery. There are exposed moves where the path is rather narrow, and one short stretch is protected with a cable. Beware of landslides and note that the route is not recommended after a spell of heavy rain. Head inland from Boca do Risco to follow a path down through a valley to end on a road at Ribeira Seca.

Start near the church in **Porto da Cruz** and cross a
cobbled bridge. Follow the road straight uphill, then turn
sharply right and left to negotiate a hairpin bend. Pass a
road junction and follow the road through a small rock
cutting, noting how bouldery the bedrock is. The cliff-
coast road offers fine views back to Porto da Cruz, then
descends into a valley. Pass a shop/**bar**, then two roads
branch off closely together to the right, so keep left to
climb uphill and round into a higher valley. Pass another
little shop/**bar** and follow the road up to the last houses.

An orange sign marks a track leading from the end
of the road. Climb gently, and avoid a track climbing
more steeply to the left. All of a sudden, pines cover a
slope dropping steeply to the sea. Look back along the
coast to Penha de Águia, but Porto da Cruz is not in sight.
At the end of the track, continue along a narrower path
on a slope of pine, laurel and heather. Be careful when
the path narrows, and at that point climb up a short rocky

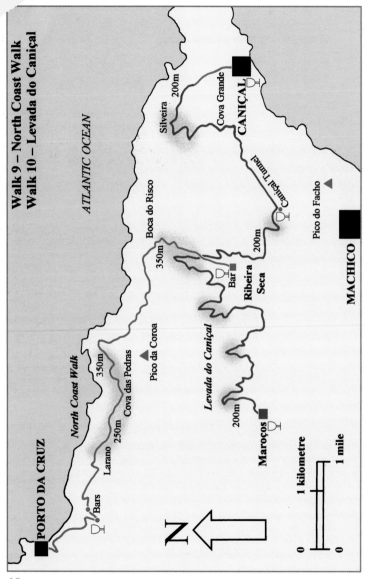

Walk 9 – North Coast Walk
Walk 10 – Levada do Caniçal

ATLANTIC OCEAN

PORTO DA CRUZ

North Coast Walk

Bars

350m
Larano
250m

Cova das Pedras
▲ Pico da Coroa

350m

Boca do Risco

Silveira
200m

CANIÇAL

Cova Grande

Caniçal Tunnel

200m

▲ Pico do Facho

MACHICO

Bar
Ribeira Seca

Levada do Caniçal

200m

Maroços

N

0   1 kilometre
0   1 mile

ramp to continue along the correct line. The other path disappears on a rather steep slope.

The path turns in and out of a handful of small gullies on the steep, wooded slope. Step down a rock outcrop and enjoy views stretching back to Porto da Cruz, and further along the coast to Santana. There are pines, mimosa and eucalyptus, but little ground cover, though there are dense heathery growths alongside the path while turning round a significant point. Enjoy views both ways for a while; back to Porto da Cruz and Santana and ahead to the Ponta de São Lourenço and the distant island of Porto Santo.

The path suddenly swings round into a huge bare hollow, where steep slopes of grass and crumbling rock fall towards the sea. Only a few small trees or clumps of heather are dotted across the slopes, and the path is narrow and crumbly in places. Beware of landslips on this stretch, and there are always rocks ready to come crashing down. Take particular care crossing a rock-wall that has a short length of cable attached. Follow the path past a little pinnacle of rock and reach a dense cover of heather, laurel, mimosa, and masses of brambles and bracken.

There are a couple open areas, but there are also patches of woodland so dense that it is quite dark inside. The path is broad and stony as it turns round a rocky headland, and there is a good view back across the most rugged part of the walk, with Santana still in view in the distance. Go through another dense patch of vegetation, turn round another headland, then continue along the path through gorse before rising gently to the **Boca do Risco.**

Enjoy the last of the cliff-coast views before following the path downhill from Boca do Risco. Although the valley seems well wooded, the stony path often crosses grassy slopes and keeps away from denser stands of trees. Heather and laurel increase in size on the way down, and there is a smallholding nearby where there may be a few animals. The path passes mimosa and tall pines and continues to descend easily, though it is rockier as it negotiates a rugged side valley. Trees give way to more

Transport:

SAM Buses 53, 56 and 78 serve Porto da Cruz. SAM Bus 113 serves Ribeira Seca.

Refreshments:

Bars and restaurants at Porto da Cruz, with a couple of small shop/bars on the way out of town. The walk ends at a bar at Ribeira Seca.

The track finally reaches the cliff line high above Porto da Cruz

cultivated slopes and there are little storage sheds below. Later, look out for the Levada do Caniçal and notice that the lower part of the valley is full of farms and houses. Cross over the levada, or alternatively, turn left and follow the levada to the Caniçal tunnel, referring to Walk 10. The path is rough and stony as it descends, with some parts under concrete, and there are street lights all the way down to **Ribeira Seca**. At the bottom, go down a flight of steps to land on the road at the **Bar** Boca do Risco.

WALK 10: Levada do Caniçal

THE ROUTE
Distance:
12 or 19km (7½ or 11¾ miles).
Start:
At the bus terminus at Maroços – 316231.
Finish:
At the Caniçal tunnel – 351226, or at Caniçal –
375232.
Maps:
Military Survey 1:25,000 Sheets 7 and 8 or
IGC 1:50,000 Madeira East.
Terrain:
The levada is practically level, but crosses steep slopes
that may be cultivated or wooded. The path beside the
levada is good, though continuing to Caniçal it
becomes more overgrown.

Leave the bus terminus at **Maroços** and walk down a road
from the Snack Bar Estevão. Cross a bridge at the bottom
and climb up a flight of steps on the right. Note that there
are two levadas on the steep slope. Cross a narrow one
after climbing 137 steps, then find the wider **Levada do
Caniçal** after climbing 223 steps. Turn right to start
walking downstream. The path is concrete as it passes
between houses above Maroços, and there are street
lights. The path is earth as it swings left into a narrow side
valley drained by the Ribeira das Cales. Leaving this
valley, enjoy a fine view down the main valley to Pico
do Facho, which rises between Machico and Caniçal.
One by one, the Ilhas Desertas sail into view out to sea.
The levada path becomes concrete again as it swings into
the next side valley, drained by the Ribeira Grande. All
kinds of fruit and vegetables grow on the terraces. Turn
round the head of the valley, then follow an earth path,
rocky in places, with mimosa growing alongside a few
pines and eucalyptus.

The Levada do Caniçal
offers a pleasant, varied
route through the
Machico valley. All
manner of fruit and
vegetables grow on the
sunny, south-facing
cultivated slopes, but
the levada also runs
into well-wooded side
valleys where there is
plenty of shade. The
trees are mostly
mimosa, though there
are also pine and
eucalyptus.
Occasionally the
levada crosses a rocky
slope, but there is little
feeling of exposure.
When the levada
reaches the Caniçal
tunnel, either finish at
that point or walk
through the tunnel and
continue further. Enjoy
a fine stretch of the
levada, but
unfortunately, the walk
passes a rubbish dump
to reach Caniçal.

Walking along the Levada do Caniçal above Maroços on a wet day

Turn round another little valley, then meander past small houses. Another rocky stretch leads past a cave and through a short tunnel. Emerge with a view of Machico and continue along the levada. Although the levada has been cut from rock, There is no real sense of exposure, despite overhanging rock above.

Turn left round a corner at a water intake building to see the next side valley. This is a big valley, drained by the Ribeira Seca. Several little side valleys are negotiated while working round the bigger valley.

The first little valley is under cultivation, while the next one is densely planted with mimosa trees. Another side valley is long and cultivated, and no habitations are in view, only small huts and plenty of fruit and vegetables. Later, overlook the bustle of the main valley leading down to Machico. When railings run beside the levada, there is a track leading down to a narrow road and a turning circle. This offers an easy exit from the walk, otherwise keep following the levada. Turn round another little valley, then turn a rocky corner into the next valley. The head of the **Ribeira Seca** is under cultivation, but also features plenty of mimosa. Lose sight of habitations again, seeing only a few little huts on the terraces, before turning sharply round the head of the valley.

Leave the head of the valley and walk along a bit of a rocky cut, then notice a path slicing downhill to the right, marked with street lights. This offers a descent to the **Bar** Boca do Risco if required. To continue along the levada, rock overhangs the channel, but there is no real sense of exposure. A pronounced left bend takes the path into a side valley where more mimosa grows. Turn round the head of the valley and proceed along a rocky cut. Follow the levada as it meanders in and out of folds on the steep valley side. There are views down the valley to Machico, but there are also wooded areas with mimosa, pine and eucalyptus. The main ER-109 road rises from Machico, and after crossing another wooded slope and passing a few houses, reach the road at the mouth of the **Caniçal Tunnel**.

Buses stop near the tunnel mouth, and it is only a short walk down to the Restaurante O Tunel for something to eat and drink. Alternatively, follow the levada to Caniçal by walking through the tunnel. Keep to the path on the left side of the tunnel, where the water is confined to a pipe. The tunnel runs for 800m (875yds) through the Pico de Nossa Senhora and it is unpleasant to share it with traffic. Although the levada runs close to the main

Transport:
SAM Bus 156 serves Maroços. SAM Bus 113 serves the Caniçal tunnel and Caniçal.

Refreshments:
There are bars at Maroços, and a bar off-route at Ribeira Seca. There is a bar near the Caniçal tunnel and several bars and restaurants in the village of Caniçal.

road, walk down the road a short way, then walk up a quarry access road on the left. Head off to the right to continue along the course of the levada. Signs warn of falling rocks from the quarry and the path is less trodden. Cling to a narrow path on a cliff, which some might find unnerving, but it gets better later. There are odd mimosa trees, prickly pears and malfurada bushes. Turn left round a rocky corner and enjoy the view to Caniçal and the Ponta de São Lourenço.

The path is a bit overgrown and brambly in places, but easy enough to follow as the levada is just alongside. After slicing across the hillside, a track crosses the levada. Enter a dense woodland of mimosa, pine, oak and eucalyptus. The levada has a red-earth bank and turns round a little valley where a small bridge is crossed with a straddling manoeuvre. The levada suddenly turns right and rushes downhill. Follow the broad track alongside and quickly leave the woods. Unfortunately, a lot of rubbish lies dumped beside the track, so it is a poor end to a good walk. The track and a road lead to a crossroads where there is a post office. Either catch a bus here, or walk further downhill and turn right to reach the centre of **Caniçal**. There is plenty of food and drink and an interesting whaling museum to visit.

Walk 11: Ponta de São Lourenço

THE ROUTE

Distance:
7km (41/4 miles) there and back.

Start/Finish:
At the end of the road at the Baia d'Abra – 410237.

Maps:
Military Survey 1:25,000 Sheet 7 or
IGC 1:50,000 Madeira East.

Terrain:
Good paths across bare hillsides and along cliff edges.
The rock is broken and crumbling in places and one
exposed stretch has safety fencing.

Start from the road-end **car park** at the Baia d'Abra, which
is occasionally served by buses. The landscape is bare,
dry, gritty, bouldery and teems with lizards. There is a
view of the lighthouse on the Ilhéu do Farol, as well as to
a pierced headland beneath the furthest hill reached on
this walk. Further out to sea are the Ilhas Desertas. Follow
a clear gravel path downhill and turn right down another
path. Pass through a tumbled wall where there is a
national park sign. The path is marked with short wooden
posts topped with white paint, and when the path
becomes vague, look ahead to spot the next post. Walk
downhill and divert a short way left to reach a cliff-top stance
where there is a view of a fine pointed sea stack, as well
as a remarkable cliff line.

Double back a short way and follow the path further
uphill to reach another fine viewpoint. White posts lead
up to the left on a crumbling rocky slope. Do not climb
to the summit of this rugged little hill, but swing right and
take care on a short, steep, rocky descent to a gap. Enjoy
more stunning views, taking in colourful, contorted,
banded cliffs, as well as a rugged stack and a distant view

The Ponta de São
Lourenço is the
shattered, battered
eastern point of
Madeira. It is a long,
rugged peninsula
where the sea has
carved rocky coves
into the cliffs and
landslips have created
jagged edges. The
further east the walk
proceeds, the more
remarkable the
scenery, but note that
there are exposed cliffs
along the way. There is
no way across the
rocky gap called the
Boqueirão, or to the
lighthouse on the Ilhéu
do Farol. The distant
continuation of the
point is seen in the
Ilhas Desertas. Turn
round and walk back
to the start at the Baia
d'Abra.

67

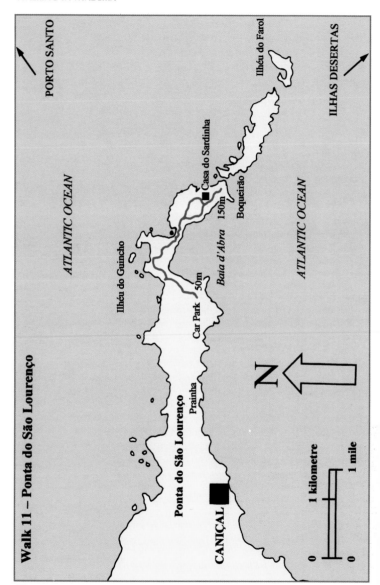

Walk 11 – Ponta do São Lourenço

of Porto Santo. Leave the gap and contour across a steep and rocky slope that needs care. Keep to the lowest path to be led onto an easier path cutting across a grassy slope.

When the terrain becomes rocky again, there is a narrow rocky edge to traverse. This is quite exposed, but there is safety fencing on both sides. When the path runs off the rocky edge onto easier ground, there is another fine view off to the left taking in more rugged cliff faces. The path contours across another slope, then there is a choice of routes marked by posts.

Keep to the left to proceed and note that there is later a diversion away from an eroded area where plants are being re-established. Walk down to a solitary house called the **Casa do Sardinha**. Palm trees around the house offer the only shade on a hot and sunny day. The house was an early 20th-century residence, reached by boat from a nearby pier. It is now used as a centre for the Reserva Natural da Ponto de São Lourenço. Follow a steep and gritty path uphill from the house, to reach two rocky little summits on top of the hill. Views extend to the Ilhéu do Farol, but walk no further in that direction because of the yawning gulf of the Boqueirão beneath your feet. Content yourself with the view, leading the eye to the Ilhas Desertas, Porto Santo and taking in much of eastern Madeira.

Retrace steps downhill, then keep left of the **Casa do Sardinha**. A path leads almost down to the rocky shore, then heads uphill and left. Rejoin the path that crosses the rocky edge with the safety fencing, and then basically retrace steps to the **Baia d'Abra**. If a bus is due, then enjoy something to eat and drink from the snack van while waiting for it. If not, then you may have to walk back along the road to Caniçal.

Transport:

SAM Bus 113 sometimes runs beyond Caniçal to the Baia d'Abra.

Refreshments:

There is often a snack van parked at the Baia d'Abra. There are also a couple of bars and restaurants back along the road to Caniçal.

Walkers leave one of the gaps on the jagged cliff line at São Lourenço

WALK 12: Pico do Areeiro to Pico Ruivo

THE ROUTE
Distance:
11km (6½ miles).
Start/Finish:
At the Pousada Areeiro – 196233.
Maps:
Military Survey 1:25,000 Sheets 5 and 6 or
IGC 1:50,000 Madeira East.
Terrain:
Mountainous, with the narrow path often cut across sheer cliffs or through six tunnels. The exposure is severe. Other parts of the path may be steep and stony, or cross bare rock. Not recommended in bad weather.

Start at the Pousada Areeiro on the summit of **Pico do Areeiro**. There is a restaurant and the Boutique Areeiro souvenir shop, as well as a large car park. A few steps lead up to a viewpoint at 1818m (5965ft), and this can be a surprisingly popular place at sunrise and sunset, when there is less likelihood of cloud cover. Start early to enjoy views before clouds build up in the afternoon. Close to the viewpoint is a sign pointing the way to Pico Ruivo. It gives the distance as 10km (6 miles), which is actually the return distance via the tunnels. Our return distance is actually 11km (6½ miles). The path is initially paved and runs gently downhill. Go through a gate on a gap and cross a small hump. The path is mostly between fences. Walk down steps to cross another gap, then slice across the rocky northern side of the ridge, where the path exploits a weak layer in the basalt. Cross a yellow grid, and make a short detour to the right to a fine viewpoint. Apart from the impressive mountain scenery, try to pick out a few stretches of the path that are used on the return journey.

One of the most popular mountain walks on Madeira is from Pico do Areeiro to Pico Ruivo. Be warned that it suffers from rockfalls and landslips, and in the past has been closed to walkers! Pico do Areeiro is the second-highest mountain on the island, yet can be reached by road, and taxi drivers take people up there for early morning sunrises. The path to Pico Ruivo leads through five tunnels and often clings precariously to narrow, unfenced ledges cut into sheer cliffs. After enjoying the view from the highest point on Madeira, return to Pico do Areeiro using a path that was the regular route before the tunnels were cut. This is rough and rocky, with plenty of ascent and descent.

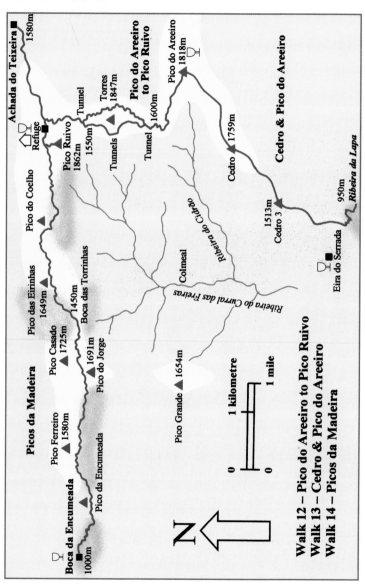

Walk 12 – Pico do Areeiro to Pico Ruivo
Walk 13 – Cedro & Pico do Areeiro
Walk 14 – Picos da Madeira

Walk back a few paces from the viewpoint and continue along the path, using steps to climb over the ridge. A path of pulverised pumice follows the crest of the ridge, where fencing protects against awesome drops. Walk down steps on a narrow part of the ridge to reach a stone-carved picnic table at another fine viewpoint. The path is fenced a short way as it climbs uphill, then it cuts across a cliff and begins to descend with a vengeance using flights of crumbling stone steps. Zig-zag beneath a wedged boulder and pass three little pinnacles of rock on the descent, then pass through a hole in a basalt dyke. The rock is much harder where a gap is crossed, then walk along a well-vegetated terrace. Go through a **tunnel** cutting straight through the rugged little Pico do Gato. There is good headroom and a torch is not needed. Another steep flight of steps run downhill and can be slippery. There are fine views of the head of the Curral valley before reaching a gap. There is a choice of paths here, so turn left to use the direct path to Pico Ruivo. The return route uses the other path, so you will be back here later in the day.

Contour across a steep slope covered in broom. Pass a couple of caves, then there is a fenced stretch of path across a sheer cliff. Be warned that the path is very narrow, very exposed, and the fencing may be in tatters. There is a short length of cable to hold onto at one stage. Go through a small rock cutting and contour across the face to reach another **tunnel**. A torch is an advantage, though not absolutely necessary, and there is good headroom. Emerge with a view of Pico Ruivo ahead, and make a sharp right turn. A short and very narrow unprotected path leads to the next short **tunnel**. Afterwards, turn immediately right through a little rock cutting to continue. Walk gently downhill and go through another short **tunnel**, then continue down to reach a rocky promontory.

This is a handy place to take a break from the exposure and narrow paths, and gaze in wonder at the steepness of the cliffs and the multi-coloured layers that make up these mountains. Notice the alternating bands of hard and soft rock, and realise that these mountains

Transport:
Nova minibuses visit the Pousada Areeiro, otherwise use a taxi.

Refreshments:
There is a restaurant at the Pousada Areeiro, and a small bar at the refuge on Pico Ruivo.

Looking down on the mountain refuge from the summit of Pico Ruivo

are always going to be prone to rockfalls and landslips, and gullies channel debris downwards. Follow the path downhill and go through a small **tunnel**. Climb uphill and negotiate a series of zig-zags to reach the final **tunnel**.

This has good headroom, and leads from one side of the ridge to the other. Go through a gate to leave the tunnel, then turn left to continue walking towards Pico Ruivo, though you will return to this point later.

The path slices across a cliff face with a fence alongside. Pass a couple of caves and turn a corner. The path passes ancient stands of tree heather, then continues round another rocky corner where the fencing ends. The path climbs through the tree heather and is paved as it zig-zags uphill. Another fenced stretch climbs further, then more zig-zags lead up through a gate. Walk further uphill to a path junction and turn left to climb up steps to the **refuge**. Refreshments can be obtained here, as well as a bed for the night!

The final push to the summit is easy. Leave the refuge to follow steps and a well-worn path further uphill. At a junction of paths, turn left again, spiral up steps and follow another worn path to the top of **Pico Ruivo**. There is a large trig point at 1862m (6109ft) and a monument. The summit is surrounded by a wooden fence and is a fine viewpoint. Look back along the rugged ridge to Pico do Areeiro, as well as down into the deep valley towards Curral das Freiras. Pico Grande is identified by its prominent summit tor, then look along the rugged crest of Madeira towards the plateau of Paúl da Serra. Densely wooded slopes fall away to the north coast and the path heading eastwards to Teixeira can be seen. Retrace steps to the refuge.

Leave the **refuge**, walk down steps to a path junction and turn right. Walk down the paved path through the tree heather and go through the gate. Zig-zag down through tree heather, and turn round a couple of rocky corners. You arrived this way, so you are just retracing steps. The path is fenced where it cuts across a cliff, passing a couple of caves and reaching a tunnel mouth. A return could be made through the **tunnel** to return to Pico do Areeiro, but there is also a path on the eastern side of the ridge, though it involves more ascent and descent than the route through the tunnels.

Follow the path away from the tunnel, sometimes with fencing alongside and sometimes without. It is less of a cliff and more of a slope, and at one point the path passes behind a wedged boulder. There is a very bendy stretch round a series of gullies, then climb and turn round stony bends. Stone steps and stony zig-zags lead higher and higher, then go through a little notch in the rock and a fenced path leads across a cliff. Go through a gate and climb a little more, then there is a descent without a fence. Go down a zig-zag flight of steep and worn stone steps, which may be slippery in places. There are two little caves at the bottom, and the path is stony as it zig-zags further down a slope of bracken and broom. There are more steep and crumbly steps, then gentler gradients. There are a couple of fenced stretches as the path levels out and begins to climb again, always cutting across a steep slope. Go through a gate on a gap and turn left to climb steep flights of steps. These were used on the outward journey and they lead up to the **tunnel** through Pico do Gato.

Emerge from the tunnel to follow a terrace path and go through a hole in a basalt dyke. Zig-zag up a crumbling flight of steps, passing three little pinnacles of rock and passing beneath a wedged boulder. At the top of the steps the path cuts across a cliff and is fenced, then it descends to reach a stone-carved picnic table at a viewpoint. Walk up steps along a narrow part of the ridge, where fencing protects against awesome drops. Follow a path of pulverised pumice along the crest, then walk down steps to leave the crest. There is a viewpoint off to the left, or simply continue across a yellow grid to return directly to Pico do Areeiro. The path exploits a weak layer in the basalt, then crosses a gap and leads up some steps. Cross a small hump and go through a gate on another gentle gap, then follow the paved path straight up to **Pico do Areeiro**.

WALK 13: Cedro and Pico do Areeiro

THE ROUTE

Distance:
6.5km (4 miles).

Start:
Ribeira da Lapa on the ER-107 road – 172198

Finish:
At the Pousada Areeiro – 196233.

Maps:
Military Survey 1:25,000 Sheets 5 and 6 or
IGC 1:50,000 Madeira East and West.

Terrain:
Mountainous, with a steep and rocky ascent with
thorny scrub gives way to a largely grassy ridge without
a clear trodden path. Higher parts are rocky.

From certain viewpoints, Cedro and Pico do Areeiro sometimes look smooth and seem to offer the promise of easy walking. The ridge falling from Cedro south-west to the Curral valley looks as though it offers easy walking. It does not, as the lower part of the ridge is steep and rugged, as well as being covered in thorny scrub, so the road cannot be reached without suffering. Other than that the walk would be splendid; downhill along a lovely grassy ridge. It is possible to reverse things and climb the steep, rugged, thorny slope first, then let the memory of it fade while enjoying the rest of the ascent to Cedro and Pico do Areeiro.

Start on the ER-107 road between Funchal and Curral das Freiras, where the road bends to cross the **Ribeira da Lapa**. There is a parking space before the bridge where the bus can stop. The altitude is 950m (3115ft). Walk across the bridge and a short way along the road towards Curral, just round the first slight bend. Chestnuts give way to tall pines on the slope above, and although there is a tall fence beside the road, local people have peeled it apart in one place. A steep path climbs uphill from this point, and its course is shown on some maps, but there was a fire on this slope and masses of thorny scrub have since obscured the line of the path. If there is no trace of the path, or if the slope proves too difficult, then turn back.

The path climbs a short way from the road, then cuts off a little to the right, becoming vague as it zig-zags uphill. Climb above the tall trees and notice that young trees have been planted in an effort to regenerate the slope. Brambles make it difficult to spot where the path swings left and cuts across the steep and rugged slope.

An evening view of Cedro's gentle slopes from Pico do Areeiro

There are fallen tree trunks, denser growths of brambles, and gorse bushes. Zig-zag further up a rocky slope, and do not pass under an electricity transmission line, but climb up to the ridge. Turn right on top to follow the narrow, rocky, steep-sided ridge northwards. While licking your wounds, enjoy fine views over the Curral valley in the knowledge that the worst is over.

There is a path along the rocky ridge passing occasional charred pines. The path peters out, so either cross over or skirt a rounded hill covered in bracken at 1400m (4595ft). There are good views over the Curral valley, with Pico Grande and its summit tor rising steep and rugged on the other side. Swing right and cross a gentle gap, then climb the next hill on the broad crest at 1456m (4777ft). There is a boundary marker on top bearing a list of towns and villages. Continue along a rounded, pathless, wonderfully grassy ridge, then walk down to a grassy gap. A line of boulders leads up to the next summit, so keep to the right of these, then switch back to the left to reach the top of **Cedro 3** at 1513m (4964ft). There is another boundary marker at this point.

Cross another little gap and climb a slope covered in boulders, giving way to bare rock on the next summit. A concrete marker stands at 1588m (5210ft). Walk across easy bedrock towards the next little gap. The next rounded hill is bare and bouldery. Either keep to the right, or climb to the summit at 1612m (5289ft). Walk down across grass and boulders to reach the corner of a drystone wall and fence, then follow these lines uphill. Next, follow the fence uphill to the left after passing a ladder stile. Reach a bouldery crest where there is another boundary marker. Either follow the fence all the way to the top of **Cedro**, or keep just to the left and boulder-hop along the crest. The summit is marked by a trig point at 1759m (5771ft), with good views of the surrounding mountains. Look along the ridge to Pico do Areeiro, and take in all the peaks round the Curral valley to Pico Grande, with Paúl da Serra and Terreiros beyond.

Walk down a slope of pulverised pumice to leave the summit of Cedro, and notice how bare the sheep-grazed slopes are on the other side of the fence. After a break of slope, the ground is bouldery across a gap. The fence leads up and along the bouldery crest to reach the next summit, which has a boundary marker at 1763m (5784ft). Follow the fence down along a bouldery, grassy crest. Cross a ladder stile at a fence junction to follow one last, short, crumbling, bouldery ridge up to a road bend, where slopes fall steep and rugged to the head of the Curral valley. Walk straight uphill from the road bend to reach the car park at the Pousada Areeiro. Climb a few steps alongside and to the **Pico do Areeiro** viewpoint at 1818m (5965ft). This can be a surprisingly popular place at sunrise and sunset, when there is less likelihood of cloud cover. Unless you can negotiate a lift or arrange to be collected on the summit, then call for a taxi to leave the mountain. Enjoy a drink and a meal in the restaurant while waiting.

Transport
Camacha Bus 81 crosses the Ribeira da Lapa. Taxi from Pico do Areeiro.

Refreshments:
There is a bar and restaurant at the Pousada Areeiro.

WALK 14: Picos da Madeira

One of the classic high-level mountain walks in Madeira runs east to west from Achada do Teixeira to the Boca da Encumeada. The ridge route crosses the highest mountain on the island, Pico Ruivo, and passes close to other summits. The path is generally quite clear and obvious. The slopes on either side are fairly open at the start, but become more and more clothed in tree heather and dense undergrowth. The advantage of walking from east to west is in losing more height than is gained, but keep an eye on the time to reach the Boca da Encumeada for the last bus

THE ROUTE
Distance:
15km (9½ miles).
Start:
Achada do Teixeira – 205265.
Finish:
Boca da Encumeada – 112255.
Maps:
Military Survey 1:25,000 Sheets 5 and 6 or IGC 1:50,000 Madeira East and West.
Terrain:
Mountainous, though the path is generally clear throughout. There are some steep and stony stretches, as well as several flights of steps, and dense vegetation cover in places. Care is needed at path junctions in mist.

Use a taxi to reach the road-end car park at **Achada do Teixeira,** around 1580m (5185ft). Views encompass the mountains, valleys and sea. Look across to Pico do Areeiro, but Pico Ruivo is not in view. Set off towards Pico Ruivo by following the clear, paved path westwards along the ridge. Zig-zag uphill and pass through a fence, then follow the path along the crest to pass a stone shelter. Walk uphill and drift to the right of the ridge to follow the path to another stone shelter, with a water source and picnic tables. Climb up steps, then walk downhill and pass a signpost for Pico Ruivo. The path crosses the ridge and passes yet another stone shelter, and there are views of the rocky ridge linking Pico Ruivo and Pico do Areeiro. Pass rocky outcrops and big boulders, then go through a gate and walk up steps on a slope of tree heather. The paved path crosses an area of bare pumice and reaches a junction. Climb up steps to the **refuge**. Refreshments can be obtained here, as well as a bed for the night!

The final push to the summit is easy. Leave the refuge to follow steps and a well-worn path further uphill. At a junction of paths, turn left again, spiral up steps and follow another worn path to the top of **Pico Ruivo**. There is a large trig point at 1862m (6109ft) and a monument. The summit is surrounded by a wooden fence and is a fine viewpoint. Look along the rugged ridge to Pico do Areeiro, as well as down into the deep valley towards Curral das Freiras. Pico Grande is identified by its prominent summit tor, then look along the rugged crest of Madeira towards the plateau of Paúl da Serra. Densely wooded slopes fall away to the north coast and the path heading eastwards to Teixeira can be seen. Retrace steps down from the summit, and turn left to walk along the main ridge.

The path wanders along the stony crest, then drifts down to the left and begins to zig-zag through thick heather. It is rough and stony underfoot, and turns round a crumbling rocky lip to go through a gate. The path is steep and rough as it descends, avoiding Pico da Lapa da Cadela, then it begins to level out before climbing though broom and heather. There are good views while turning round a corner flanked by broom, then go through another gate. Climb up a rugged path on a wooded slope and turn round an open corner below **Pico do Coelho**.

The path rises and falls, then climbs gently to cut back and forth across the main ridge. Rocky zig-zags lead down to a gap. Continue across a wooded slope, then slice down across a heathery slope. Turn round a rocky corner and avoid a path heading off down to the left. Keep right and follow the higher path through tree heather to cross the ridge again, between **Pico das Eirinhas** and Pico da Laje. Descend from the ridge, walking down stone steps to follow a narrow, well-vegetated path. Steep flights of stone steps lead back up towards the ridge, and there are a couple of caves in a nearby cliff. The path undulates along the ridge and there is an open corner where there are views on both sides. Walk through a well-wooded, heathery patch, then continue down steps and a rocky ramp to land on the **Boca das Torrinhas** at 1450m (4760ft). There are big signposts here.

Transport:
Taxi to Achada do Teixeira. Rodoeste Bus 6 and 139 serve Boca da Encumeada.

Refreshments:
There is a small bar at the refuge on Pico Ruivo. The Snack Bar Restaurante Encumeada is at the end of the walk.

Climbing steps through tree heather to reach the refuge on Pico Ruivo

Head westwards up a flight of stone steps, continuing on a gentler path that crosses the ridge. A more rugged path and zig-zag steps lead up to a higher gap, more like a rocky cleft full of ferns and exotic plants. Squeeze between the rocks and follow the path downhill a short way. It levels out and begins to climb on a slope of dense heather, but is rather narrow and worn as it zig-zags up to a cave. Continue climbing along an easier zig-zag path, where the stones underfoot make musical chinking sounds. Pass a blade-like outcrop of rock to reach a gritty gap between **Pico Casado** and Pico do Jorge.

The path descends from the ridge and goes down steps on the flanks of **Pico do Jorge**, into dense tree heather and bilberry. Follow the path onwards and there is a cave off to the left. On a more open part of the ridge, a path on the left offers a rugged route to Pico Grande. Staying on the main path, however, there is broom and heather on a narrow part of the ridge. A rugged path descends through dense heather and there is a view of the jagged rocky ridge of Pico Ferreiro ahead. Walk down rock steps and the path slips left of the ridge to avoid rocky pinnacles.

A zig-zag path leads away from the ridge and down a wooded slope through a gate. Drop down to follow a path that exploits a crumbling layer below a cliff on the southern flank of **Pico Ferreiro**. Go through another gate while following this path, passing tall tree heather and ancient tils on the slope beneath the cliff. At an open corner, enjoy views of the surrounding mountains, and in particular Pico Grande, then continue through tall tree heather to make your way across a slope and down rugged steps. Pass a spring called the Fonte do Pico do Ferreiro among the trees. The path crosses a heathery slope, turning right, then swinging left, to go down more steps. Pass a small cave on the descent, then the path slices off to the left, down steps and through a gate to land on a gap.

The gap is narrow and well vegetated. Climb up steps to leave it, then keep left to traverse a steep slope covered in broom, passing below **Pico da Encumeada**. Cross a bare shoulder offering good views, then follow the path down along a ridge of broom, heather and bilberry, enjoying the views. Steep flights of stone steps follow, and they may be slippery. Often, they are substantially buttressed, but sometimes the path is narrow and flanked by a tangle of vegetation, including bracken and brambles. Of particular note are the lily of the valley trees. At the bottom of the steps, continue down the path, then down a track that serves a prominent mast. Reach the road at the **Boca da Encumeada** and turn left to pass through a rock cutting to reach the Snack Bar Restaurante Encumeada.

Walk 15 – Corticeiras to Boca da Encumeada
Walk 16 – Boca da Corrida to Curral das Freiras
Walk 17 – Boca da Encumeada to Curral das Freiras
Walk 18 – Corticeiras to Curral das Freiras

Walk 15: Corticeiras to Boca da Encumeada

The Route
Distance:
17km (10½ miles).
Start:
Corticeiras – 135180.
Finish:
Boca da Encumeada – 112255.
Maps:
Military Survey 1:25,000 Sheets 5 and 8 or
IGC 1:50,000 Madeira West.
Terrain:
A road is used for the ascent, then fairly good mountain paths are followed, though these are steep and rocky in places. The slopes are more wooded towards the end.

This walk leads through the mountains from one high gap to another. Climb from Corticeiras to the Boca da Corrida, then pick a way across the flanks of mountains such as Pico do Serradinho and Pico Grande, to reach the Boca da Encumeada. There are notable mountain viewpoints along the way, though there is no need to climb any peaks to enjoy them. There is also the danger of rockfalls while crossing the steep and rocky flanks of Pico Grande. Generally, the path runs downhill and around the foot of Pico Grande, traversing a well-wooded valley before climbing up to the Boca da Encumeada.

Start in **Corticeiras**, where the Estrada Jardim da Serra is the road that leads uphill from the village. This road climbs steeply and becomes the Estrada da Corrida. The Snack **Bar** Mercearia Tibúrcio and Delta Mini Mercado and **Bar** offer refreshments on the ascent, and a break is welcome on a hot day. There is a local bus service, not shown on any timetables, that runs up and down the road on odd occasions. Pass the last houses on the road and continue up through a valley dominated by chestnut, with some pine and eucalyptus. Cross a cattle grid, then the road is bendy and attractively cobbled. It ends at the Posto Florestal Jardim da Serra, where there is a small car park and picnic site, around 1220m (4000ft). There is a shrine to São Cristovão in the shade of a few trees. Splendid views take in mountains from Pico Grande to Pico Ruivo and Pico do Areeiro, while Curral das Freiras lies deep in the valley. Some walkers prefer to hire a taxi from Estreito de Câmara de Lobos to reach the **Boca da Corrida**. Taking a taxi to this point saves 3.5km (2 miles).

An easy mountain path picks a way round Pico do Serradinho

Follow a track uphill through chained pillars, where a steep path rising to the right is signposted for Curral das Freiras and Encumeada. The path levels out and crosses a slope covered in broom, dotted with a few chestnuts. Enjoy superb views as the track gradually descends, then steeper zig-zags lead to a gap called the **Boca dos Corgos**, where there are more chestnuts. The path slices across the rocky slopes of Pico do Cavalo, where there is less broom, but a mixture of other shrubs. The path is cut from rock or buttressed as it climbs, with fine mountain views. After wriggling across the ridge the path descends to a gap at **Passo de Ares**, then a level stretch goes through a gateway. Climb and contour round the slopes of **Pico do Serradinho**, where there are interesting corners to turn and more good views. There is chestnut and deep heather, then the path moves onto a ridge covered in gorse scrub. Keep to the left, as paths to the right head for Pico Grande and Curral das Freiras.

Follow the path onwards, leaving the gorse and descending a rather wet slope. Cut across a cliff face below Pico Grande on a drier path and beware of rockfalls. There are other wet and muddy parts and it can be slippery in places, with masses of vegetation. The path is cut from the rock again and paved with stone in places. Stay alert to the dangers of rockfalls. The path passes some old tils and descends through tree heather. Pass round the base of a monstrous tower of rock. Keep walking round an awesome hollow on the flank of the mountain. There is a short path to the left, down through broom, to a viewpoint. Pick a way round another steep-sided hollow on the mountainside. The path follows a line of weakness between two cliff faces, descending steadily. There is a short length of drystone wall, then the stony path descends and is flanked by bracken, broom and brambles. Enjoy views of the valley and mountains, as the path turns a corner where broom scrub grows. Pick a way down beneath a frowning rock face into tall eucalyptus and swing right. There are occasional views as the path undulates through denser woodlands, passing a small building. An arched stone bridge spans a rocky gorge at the head of the valley, where there are cultivated slopes and plenty of chestnuts.

Follow the stone-paved path away from the head of the valley, through shady woods. Descend gently through pines, also looking out for eucalyptus, candleberry and bilberry. There is a rickety footbridge over a bouldery streambed, then the path passes cultivation terraces and reaches more woodland shade. Cross a slope of bracken and brambles with open views, then reach a streambed shaded with laurels. Climb the slope, crossing a handful of rocky streambeds and passing stands of eucalyptus and other trees. Reach a pipeline that feeds the generating station at Serra de Água. Walk underneath it and continue along the path. Further along the slope, the track broadens and the slopes are covered in laurel, heather, broom and brambles. The road is reached at a bend, so follow it uphill and round to the right to reach the **Boca da Encumeada**, where there is a snack bar offering refreshments.

Transport:
Rodoeste Bus 96 serves Corticeiras. Rodoeste Bus 6 and 139 serve the Boca da Encumeada.

Refreshments:
The Snack Bar Mercearia Tibúrcio and Delta Mini Mercado and Bar are passed on the ascent from Corticeiras. The Snack Bar Restaurante Encumeada is at the end of the walk.

WALK 16: Boca da Corrida to Curral das Freiras

It is possible to walk from the Boca da Corrida, along a mountain ridge, then descend a zig-zag path into the Curral valley. It is also possible to complete a more strenuous and challenging walk by climbing Pico Grande and continuing to Pico do Jorge, then walk to the Boca das Torrinhas before making a descent into the valley. Make no mistake, this is a rough, tough walk with vague paths and a danger of rockfalls in places. The route offers a link with the main mountain ridge on Madeira and could be extended to Pico Ruivo. It is even possible to complete a vast horseshoe walk round the Curral valley to reach Pico do Areeiro.

THE ROUTE
Distance:
16km (10 miles).
Start:
On the Boca da Corrida above Corticeiras – 142206.
Finish:
At the church in Curral das Freiras – 161216.
Maps:
Military Survey 1:25,000 Sheet 5 or
IGC 1:50,000 Madeira West.
Terrain:
Mountainous, with clear paths used at the start. The summit of Pico Grande requires easy scrambling on rock. A very rough, rocky path leads on, ending with an easier descent on a well-wooded, clear and obvious zig-zag path.

It is possible to use a bus to reach Corticeiras, then walk up the road to the **Boca da Corrida**, but it is a steep road. Refer to Walk 15 for details. A taxi can be hired near the church at Estreito de Câmara de Lobos to reach the high gap more quickly. The last part of the road is cobbled and leads to a small car park at the Posto Florestal Jardim da Serra around 1220m (4000ft). There are picnic tables and a shrine to São Cristovão in the shade of a few trees. Splendid views take in mountains from Pico Grande to Pico Ruivo and Pico do Areeiro, while Curral das Freiras lies deep in the valley.

Follow a track uphill through chained pillars, where a steep path rising to the right is signposted for Curral das Freiras and Encumeada. The path levels out and crosses a slope covered in broom, dotted with a few chestnuts. Enjoy superb views as the track gradually descends, then steeper zig-zags lead to a gap called the **Boca dos Corgos**, where there are more chestnuts. The path slices across the rocky slopes of Pico do Cavalo, where there is less broom, but a mixture of other shrubs. The path is cut from rock or buttressed as it climbs, with fine mountain views. After wriggling across the ridge the path descends to a gap at **Passo de Ares**, then a level stretch goes through a gateway. Climb and contour round the slopes of **Pico do Serradinho**, where there are interesting corners to turn and more good views. There is chestnut and deep heather, then the path moves onto a ridge covered in gorse scrub. Turn right uphill, through a gate on the crest, then turn left at a red sign to leave the path and climb up to a sheepfold in the shade of chestnuts on the crest. (The other path, incidentally, leads down into the Curral valley and is used in Walk 17.)

Climb above the sheepfold, passing another red sign and a cave. A cable is fixed to the rock where exposed steps rise on a steep and rocky slope. Go through a small gate and follow a reasonably clear zig-zag path, marked with paint and small cairns. There are odd chestnuts on the steep and grassy slopes, and the path passes through a little valley full of broom. Keep zig-zagging uphill, with a view of the serrated rocky crest high above. Swing well to the left, then walk up to the shattered ridge and scramble to the summit. A zig-zag cable leads to the highest peak and the **Pico Grande** summit stands at 1654m (5426ft). Views stretch from the plateau of Paúl da Serra, along the mountain crest to Pico Ruivo and Pico do Areeiro, with the Curral valley far below, and Funchal in the distance.

Retrace steps down from the rocky ridge until you are below the serrated rocky crest again, then cut off to the left following a less clear path. This crosses a gap where there is a bouldery dry-stone wall. Cross the wall and look carefully for the path, which bears left into an area of rocks and boulders. A short flight of stone steps climb uphill to confirm the route. On the other side, stone steps and broken steps plummet downhill and need great care as there is so much loose rock. Watch very carefully for the line of the path, which passes beneath towering,

Transport:
Taxi to Boca da Corrida. Camacha Bus 81 serves Curral das Freiras.

Refreshments:
There are bars and restaurants at the end in Curral das Freiras.

The jagged peaks of Torres seen on the descent to the Curral valley

overhanging cliffs. The path is vague, but needs to be spotted before continuing. Broom scrub obscures the line in places, then climb past some dead, blasted trees. Turn round a rocky corner for views of a rugged gap with Pico do Jorge beyond. Walk down past more blasted trees and short broom scrub, then pass below a gap. Go through a gate into a well-wooded area of tils and tree heather. There are a couple of open views as the path undulates across the slope. There is a towering peak of rock ahead as the path levels out. Climb up steps and steep, stony slopes, leaving the tils and tree heather to climb a well-buttressed flight of steps. The zig-zag path climbing higher is very loose and worn, the steps are crumbling, and there is a danger of rockfalls from the cliff above. Notice how sheep and goats favour the area, which is thick with their droppings. The way appears to be blocked by a fence, but look carefully to spot where to climb it. Stone steps on the other side confirm the route. Zig-zag up through tree heather, which gives way to broom as the path gains the high crest.

Turn right along a clearer path at a sign, then keep left as marked to continue along the path. Tree heather and bilberry flank the path and there is a cave off to the right. Climb up steps and continue rising on the slopes of Pico do Jorge to reach a gritty gap between **Pico Casado** and **Pico do Jorge**. Descend past a blade-like outcrop of rock, walking on stones that make a musical chinking sound. Zig-zag down to a cave, then continue down a steeper, narrower and more worn zig-zag path into dense heather. The path levels out, then climbs to a gap in the ridge; rather like a rocky cleft full of ferns and exotic plants. Squeeze between the rocks and walk down zig-zag steps and a rugged path, then a gentler path crosses back over the ridge. A flight of steps leads down to the **Boca das Torrinhas** at 1450m (4760ft), where there are big signposts.

Follow the path signposted for Curral das Freiras, which is narrow and slices across a rocky slope. It can be grassy, stony or rocky and parts of the path are buttressed and paved. There are views back to Pico Grande and its summit tor, as well as down through the Curral valley. Descend through tree heather, then emerge on another open slope with views. There is a dense stand of eucalyptus, then another open area with views. There are a few chestnuts among the eucalyptus, as well as charred and fallen pine trunks. Continue zig-zagging downhill to find some pines are still growing. There are views of houses at the head of the Curral valley, with Pico Ruivo and other peaks rising high above. Take care on the lower zig-zags and do not be tempted to short-cut. Emerge from the woods and follow the path down past cultivation terraces. It is still steep, rough and stony, but soon leads down to a concrete bridge crossing a river.

Climb up a few steps, then turn right to walk down the road through the Curral valley. There is a small **bar** near a bridge and a few houses, while the road descends to a junction beside another bridge at **Colmeal**. There are bus stops, but buses do not come late in the evening, so check the bus timetables. Walk along the road to Curral das Freiras, then continue gently downhill to cross a bridge over the Ribeira do Cidrão, then rise through two tunnels to reach **Curral das Freiras**. The first two bars are the Snack Bar A Flor do Curral and Bar O Moinho, though there are others down the road near the church.

17: Boca da Encumeada to Curral das Freiras

This walk through the mountains steers clear of the peaks, but still includes good views of them from various vantage points and high gaps. Leaving the Boca da Encumeada, the route makes its way round a well-wooded valley and gradually picks its way up and across the slopes of Pico Grande. Beware of rockfalls as some of the slopes are steep and unstable. After reaching a high gap, the route starts zig-zagging down a steep and rugged slope into the Curral valley. Although the descent is rough and stony, the path is well graded considering the steepness of the slope. It is not a path anyone would want to ascend!

THE ROUTE

Distance:
9km (5½ miles).

Start:
Boca da Encumeada – 112255.

Finish:
At the church in Curral das Freiras – 161216.

Maps:
Military Survey 1:25,000 Sheet 5 or IGC 1:50,000 Madeira West.

Terrain:
Mountainous, with well-vegetated paths used at first, and the danger of rockfalls at a higher level. The descent is along a clear, steep and stony path.

Start at the Snack Bar Restaurante **Encumeada**, where there are fine views and a chance to obtain refreshments. Walk down the road towards Serra de Água, turning left round a bend, then take a track on the left at the next bend. Laurel, heather, broom and brambles grow on the slopes, then the track narrows and at one bend there is a fine view of Pico Grande. The pipeline feeding the generating station at Serra de Água is prominently in view, so walk towards it and pass underneath it. Walk down a slope mainly covered in eucalyptus, though there are other trees too, and cross a handful of rocky streambeds. The last of these is shaded with laurels. Cross a slope of bracken and brambles with open views. More woodland shade follows, then the path passes cultivation terraces and reaches a rickety footbridge over a bouldery streambed. Climb gently through pines, but look out for eucalyptus, candleberry and bilberry. There is good shade as the stone-paved path leads to the head of the valley. There are cultivated slopes, plenty of chestnuts, and an arched stone bridge spans a rocky gorge.

The path passes a small building and undulates, sometimes in dense woods and sometimes with views across the valley. Swing left through tall eucalyptus and pick a way beneath a frowning rock face, climbing and emerging on a corner where broom scrub grows. There are good views of the valley and mountains, then climb further on the stony path, which is flanked by bracken, broom and brambles, with a short length of drystone wall. The path climbs steadily, passing only a few trees, picking out a line of weakness between two cliff faces. Work round a steep-sided hollow on the flank of Pico Grande. Also note a path to the right, down through broom, to a viewpoint.

Keep walking along the main path round into another awesome hollow on the flank of Pico Grande. Pass round the base of a monstrous tower of rock. The path climbs through tree heather and passes some old tils. There is rockfall debris on the slopes. Parts of the path are paved with stone, or cut from the rock, and some stretches are wet and muddy. It can be slippery in places, with masses of vegetation growing where there is more water. Stay alert to the danger of rockfalls as a drier path cuts across the next cliff face. There is another wet ascent, then the path levels out on a slope of gorse. There is a fine view ahead to Pico do Serradinho, and although it is possible to continue in that direction to Corticeiras, turn left uphill for Curral das Freiras. There is a gate on the crest, and anyone wanting to extend this walk by climbing **Pico Grande** can refer to Walk 16 or Walk 19 for details.

The path descends fairly gently from the gap, with good views into the Curral valley. There is a pinnacle of rock off to the right, and views of the peaks across the valley include Pico Ruivo and Pico do Areeiro. A few chestnuts offer shade on the slope, then the path goes down through a gateway and crosses a bouldery streambed. Go up through another gateway, round a corner, then zig-zag down a steep spur at Eirado. It is a well-engineered track, carved from rock or stoutly buttressed, but often stony underfoot. Chestnut woods clothe the slopes, though there are other trees too. The zig-zag path should be followed faithfully downhill, and there is a good view back up the mountainside from well

Transport:
Rodoeste Bus 6 and 139 serve the Boca da Encumeada. Camacha Bus 81 serves Curral das Freiras.

Refreshments:
The Snack Bar Restaurante Encumeada is at the start. There are bars and restaurants at the end in Curral das Freiras.

Looking along the rugged ridge from Pico Grande to Pico do Jorge

down the slope. Go through a gateway on an open slope, then there are tall chestnuts, eucalyptus and pines. Watch carefully for the zig-zag path, which later swings well to the right to continue its descent. Cultivated plots are passed, then the path reaches a road, which is followed downhill between houses to a bus stop at **Fajã Escura**.

If a bus is due, then wait here, otherwise walk to Curral das Freiras. Turn right and continue down a tarmac and concrete road, then a steeper stone track and steps lead down a wooded slope. There are street lights alongside. A bridge spans the bouldery Ribeira do Curral and once across, a path and steps lead up to the road. There is a bus stop here, otherwise keep walking to Curral. Cross a bridge over the Ribeira do Cidrão, then rise through two **tunnels** to reach **Curral das Freiras**. The first two bars are the Snack Bar A Flor do Curral and Bar O Moinho, though there are others down the road near the church.

WALK 18: Corticeiras to Curral das Freiras

THE ROUTE
Distance:
9km (5½ miles).
Start:
Near the school in Corticeiras – 137178.
Finish:
At the church in Curral das Freiras – 161216.
Maps:
Military Survey 1:25,000 Sheets 5 and 8 or IGC 1:50,000 Madeira West.
Terrain:
Wooded slopes. A clear track is used for the ascent and a steep and stony zig-zag path is used on the descent. Roads and steps are used at the end.

Start at a road junction in **Corticeiras** where there is a signpost for the Boca dos Namorados. The Bar Bilhares Pestana and Bar Bilhar Bica stand either side of the junction and there is a school situated above. If arriving on the bus that reaches Corticeiras via Fontes, get off earlier at a junction with a cobbled road signposted for the Boca dos Namorados. Follow the road uphill from Corticeiras, and turn left up this cobbled road, which is called the Estrada da Boca dos Namorados. It leads up past a few houses and terraces, passing eucalyptus and a few chestnuts. At a rough road junction the Boca dos Namorados is signposted steeply uphill as a strip of concrete, but it is better to walk along the level dirt road, which is the Estrada da Boca dos Namorados, and climb more leisurely.

Follow the dirt road up through eucalyptus and a few pines, and avoid turnings to right and left. Keep to the broad, clear dirt road that has street lights alongside. Odd

The walk from Corticeiras over the Boca dos Namorados to Curral das Freiras lets you experience the scale and depth of the Curral valley. It is an easy ascent to the Boca dos Namorados, using a broad and clear track. The descent into the Curral valley is along a steep and stony zig-zag path, often on a wooded slope, with some good views of the valley and surrounding peaks. Either stop at a road-end at Lombo Chão, where the bus turns, or follow the road across the valley and climb up to Curral das Freiras. Finishing early saves nearly 3km (2 miles) from the overall distance.

A view across the Curral valley, showing the road the bus uses!

buildings stand nearby and the track passes eucalyptus, pine and mimosa. There is a wide loop round a cultivated hollow as the track climbs above a **quarry**. Keep winding uphill through eucalyptus on the broadest and clearest track, avoiding other tracks. Pass a stand of chestnuts and the track begins to level out, reaching a junction on a gap. There is a view down between trees to Curral das Freiras, its steep-sided valley, and the peaks ranged all around. Take a break before the descent.

From the **Boca dos Namorados** keep to the track overlooking the valley as it descends gently at first. When it steepens it zig-zags and becomes stony on a very steep slope, though trees prevent any sense of exposure. The trees are eucalyptus and pine, with a few chestnuts. The path zig-zags down, then climbs a little to reach a gap where an electricity pylon stands beside **Pico do Cedro**. Despite the intrusion, there is a good view to the head of the valley, taking in surrounding peaks. Continue the descent with more steep zig-zags, which are rocky and stony underfoot. Pass clumps of laurel, broom, gorse and brambles on an open slope with good views. The path levels out a little as it passes an isolated knoll where chestnuts grow.

Zig-zag down among tall eucalyptus and pine, then continue down a densely wooded slope of laurel and chestnut. The lower parts of the path have cobbled steps and mimosa grows alongside. Swing into a damp little valley and cross a streambed, then follow a narrow concrete path uphill a short way. Prickly pears grow on a rocky slope and a few houses are reached at the road-end at **Lombo Chão**. Either wait for a bus, or if one is not due for a while, walk along the road. There are good views across to Curral das Freiras. There are sweeping loops along the road, but look carefully to spot short-cuts down flights of steps with street lights alongside. The **Bar La Truta** is reached near a bridge over the bouldery Ribeira do Curral das Freiras. Climb up the other side of the valley and the road rises in loops, crossing the Levada do Curral, passing a path that zig-zags up to Eira do Serrado. The road levels out in **Curral das Freiras**, where shops, bars and restaurants are clustered near the church.

Transport:
Rodoeste Bus 96 serves Corticeiras. Camacha Bus 81 serves Lombo Chão and Curral das Freiras.

Refreshments:
The Bar Bilhares Pestana and Bar Bilhar Bica are at Corticeiras. The Bar La Truta is deep in the Curral valley. There are bars and restaurants at the end in Curral das Freiras.

Walk 19 – Boca da Encumeada & Pico Grande
Walk 20 – Curral das Freiras to Boaventura

160m ■ Bar
Fronte

Falca do Baixo ■

Ribeira do Porco

N

Curral das Freiras to Boaventura

Lombo do Urzal ■ 450m

Levada

Ribeira do Urzal

Ribeira Grande

Pinnacles

Pico das Eirinh
▲ 1649m

Boca da Encumeada & Pico Grande

Pico Ferreiro
▲ 1580m

Pico Casado
▲ 1725m

Boca da Encumeada
1000m ■

Pico do Jorge
▲ 1691m

Boca das Torrinhas
1450m

Pico da Encumeada ▲

Poço

▲ 1455m
Pico das Empenas

670m

Bar

Colmeal

Pico Grande
1654m ▲

1250m

Boca do Cerro
1300m

Fajã Escura ■

0   1 kilometre

0   1 mile

Tunnels

CURRAL DAS FREIRAS ■ 650m

Walk 19: Boca da Encumeada and Pico Grande

THE ROUTE

Distance:
9km (5½ miles).

Start/Finish:
Boca da Encumeada – 112255.

Maps:
Military Survey 1:25,000 Sheet 5 or
IGC 1:50,000 Madeira West.

Terrain:
Mountainous, with rugged and well-vegetated paths at first, and the danger of rockfalls at a higher level. The summit of Pico Grande requires easy scrambling on rock. A very rough, rocky path leads on, then an easier path returns to the Boca da Encumeada.

There is a rugged mountain circuit that can be enjoyed from the Boca da Encumeada, taking in the summits of Pico Grande and passing close to other summits on the main mountain crest of Madeira. The walk starts by picking its way across steep, rugged, vegetated slopes, subject to rockfalls in places. Climb to the summit of Pico Grande and enjoy the view in clear weather. A rough and rocky path picks its way to the main mountain crest near Pico do Jorge. It needs care as it is vague in places, may be overgrown and is subject to rockfalls. A good mountain path runs from Pico do Jorge to Pico Ferreiro to return to the Boca da Encumeada.

Start at the Snack Bar Restaurante **Encumeada**, where there are fine views and a chance to obtain refreshments. Walk down the road towards Serra de Água, turning left round a bend, then take a track on the left at the next bend. Laurel, heather, broom and brambles grow on the slopes, then the track narrows and at one bend there is a fine view of Pico Grande. The pipeline feeding the generating station at Serra de Água is prominently in view, so walk towards it and pass underneath it. Walk down a slope mainly covered in eucalyptus, though there are other trees too, and cross a handful of rocky streambeds. The last of these is shaded with laurels. Cross a slope of bracken and brambles with open views. More woodland shade follows, then the path passes cultivation terraces and reaches a rickety footbridge over a bouldery streambed. Climb gently through pines, but look out for eucalyptus, candleberry, bilberry. There is good shade as the stone-paved path leads to the head of the valley. There are cultivated slopes, plenty of chestnuts, and an arched stone bridge spans a rocky gorge.

Transport:
Rodoeste Bus 6 and 139
serve the Boca da
Encumeada.

Refreshments:
The Snack Bar
Restaurante Encumeada
is at the start/finish.

The path passes a small building and undulates, sometimes in dense woods and sometimes with views across the valley. Swing left through tall eucalyptus and pick a way beneath a frowning rock face, climbing and emerging on a corner where broom scrub grows. There are good views of the valley and mountains, then climb further on the stony path, which is flanked by bracken, broom and brambles, with a short length of drystone wall. The path climbs steadily, passing only a few trees, picking out a line of weakness between two cliff faces. Work round a steep-sided hollow on the flank of Pico Grande. Also note a path to the right, down through broom, to a viewpoint.

Keep walking along the main path round into another awesome hollow on the flank of Pico Grande. Pass round the base of a monstrous tower of rock. The path climbs through tree heather and passes some old tils. There is rockfall debris on the slopes. Parts of the path are paved with stone, or cut from the rock, and some stretches are wet and muddy. It can be slippery in places, with masses of vegetation growing where There is more water. Stay alert to the danger of rockfalls as a drier path cuts across the next cliff face. There is another wet ascent, then the path levels out on a slope of gorse. There is a fine view ahead to Pico do Serradinho, but turn left uphill through a gate on the crest, then turn left at a red sign to leave the path and climb up to a sheepfold in the shade of chestnuts on the crest.

Climb above the sheepfold, passing another red sign and a cave. A cable is fixed to the rock where exposed steps rise on a steep and rocky slope. Go through a small gate and follow a reasonably clear zig-zag path, marked with paint and small cairns. There are odd chestnuts on the steep and grassy slopes, and the path passes through a little valley full of broom. Keep zig-zagging uphill, with a view of the serrated rocky crest high above. Swing well to the left, then walk up to the shattered ridge and scramble to the summit. A zig-zag cable leads to the highest peak and the **Pico Grande** summit stands at 1654m (5426ft). Views stretch from the plateau of Paúl da Serra, along the mountain crest to Pico Ruivo and Pico

Mist swathes the peaks on the descent of the Boca de Encumeada

do Areeiro, with the Curral valley far below, and Funchal in the distance.

Retrace steps down from the rocky ridge until you are below the serrated rocky crest again, then cut off to the left following a less clear path. This crosses a gap where there is a bouldery dry-stone wall. Cross the wall and look carefully for the path, which bears left into an area of rocks and boulders. A short flight of stone steps climb uphill to confirm the route. On the other side, stone steps and broken steps plummet downhill and need great care as there is so much loose rock. Watch very carefully for the line of the path, which passes beneath towering, overhanging cliffs. The path is vague, but needs to be spotted before continuing. Broom scrub obscures the line in places, then climb past some dead, blasted trees. Turn round a rocky corner for views of a rugged gap with **Pico do Jorge** beyond. Walk down past more blasted trees and short broom scrub, then pass below a gap. Go through a gate into a well-wooded area of tils and tree heather. There are a couple of open views as the path undulates across the slope. There is a towering peak of rock ahead as the path levels out. Climb up steps and steep, stony slopes, leaving the tils and tree heather to climb a well-buttressed flight of steps. The zig-zag path climbing higher is very loose and worn, the steps are crumbling, and there is a danger of rockfalls from the cliff above. Notice how sheep and goats favour the area, which is thick with their droppings. The way appears to be blocked by a fence, but look carefully to spot where to climb it. Stone steps on the other side confirm the route. Zig-zag up through tree heather, which gives way to broom as the path gains the high crest.

Turn left along a clearer path, where there is broom and heather on a narrow part of the ridge. A rugged path descends through dense heather and There is a view of the jagged rocky ridge of Pico Ferreiro ahead. Walk down rock steps and the path slips left of the ridge to avoid rocky pinnacles.

A zig-zag path leads away from the ridge and down a wooded slope through a gate. Drop down to follow a path that exploits a crumbling layer below a cliff on the southern flank of **Pico Ferreiro**. Go through another gate while following this path, passing tall tree heather and ancient tils on the slope beneath the cliff. At an open corner, enjoy views of the surrounding mountains, and in particular Pico Grande, then continue through tall tree heather to make your way across a slope and down rugged steps. Pass a spring called the Fonte do Pico do Ferreiro among the trees. The path crosses a heathery slope, turning right, then swinging left, to go down more steps. Pass a small cave on the descent, then the path slices off to the left, down steps and through a gate to land on a gap.

The gap is narrow and well vegetated. Climb up steps to leave it, then keep left to traverse a steep slope covered in broom, passing below **Pico da Encumeada**. Cross a bare shoulder offering good views, then follow the path down along a ridge of broom, heather and bilberry, enjoying the views. Steep flights of stone steps follow, and they may be slippery. Often, they are substantially buttressed, but sometimes the path is narrow and flanked by a tangle of vegetation, including bracken and brambles. Of particular note are the lily of the valley trees. At the bottom of the steps, continue down the path, then down a track that serves a prominent mast. Reach the road at the **Boca da Encumeada** and turn left to pass through a rock cutting to reach the Snack Bar Restaurante Encumeada.

WALK 20: Curral das Freiras to Boaventura

THE ROUTE
Distance:
13km (8 miles).
Start:
At Colmeal in the Curral valley – 158233.
Finish:
At the Bar Fronteira near Boaventura – 162310.
Maps:
Military Survey 1:25,000 Sheets 2 and 5 or IGC
1:50,000 Madeira West.
Terrain:
Roads are used at the beginning and end of the walk,
with zig-zag mountain paths and tracks in between. The
mountain slopes are largely covered in dense woodland
and paths are steep and stony or slippery in places.

Buses serving **Curral das Freiras** usually detour up the valley to a road bridge at Colmeal. Do not cross the bridge, but start walking steeply up a road towards the head of the Curral valley. Notice the big boulders in the riverbed. Climb past a few houses and a small **bar**, then watch carefully for a red arrow painted on a boulder, pointing left down some steps to reach a concrete bridge over the river. Rocky mountains tower high above; from Pico Grande to Pico do Jorge and the rugged flanks of Torres. The path climbing from the bridge is waymarked and steps lead past cultivation terraces. Zig-zag uphill into tall eucalyptus.

Roads are eating their way into mountain valleys in Madeira. For the most part they are based on old tracks routed to serve communities at the remote valley heads. Beyond the last habitations, the old mountain paths remain intact, and the zig-zag route from Curral das Freiras to Boaventura is a fine walk over the mountains. The path exploits a gap called the Boca das Torrinhas, around 1450m (4760ft). The ascent from the Curral valley is along a clear zig-zag track and path, while the descent to Lombo do Urzal is narrower, less trodden and needs care. The northern slopes are covered in dense 'cloud forest'.

The little village of Falca de Baixo is passed near the end of the walk

A stony, grooved path climbs relentlessly uphill, and this can prove difficult on a hot day, though there is the shade of the trees. The zig-zag path is usually in the woods, but occasionally emerges with a view over the rugged valley head and peaks. Waymarks help if there is another path heading off, but always keep to the clearest path to climb uphill. A few charred pines and plenty of fallen pine trunks are found among the eucalyptus, pointing to a serious blaze in the past on this slope. Climb past a few chestnuts in the dense eucalyptus, then cross a grassy slope offering fine views. Tree heather and broom grows here. Head back into another dense stand of eucalyptus. Zig-zag out into another open area, then continue climbing up a slope of tree heather. Occasionally there are views of Pico Grande and its summit tor, as well as down through the Curral valley. The path narrows as it crosses a steep slope, and it can be grassy, stony or rocky. Parts of the path are buttressed and paved approaching the **Boca das Torrinhas** at 1450m (4760ft). There are big signposts here.

Take a break, then cross over the gap and descend from the lowest point, signposted for Lombo do Urzal. Note the immediate change in character, as the path is narrow, grassy and overgrown, and sense the transition from dry air to moist air while crossing the ridge. The path is well engineered in places, but little used, so watch for painted waymarks. Sometimes it is not possible to see ahead for more than a few paces through dense tree heather, laurel, bilberry and flowery undergrowth. There is also bracken and brambles, and the path may be routed across soft and crumbling earth. Climb from time to time as the path negotiates a steep and densely wooded valley head below Pico da Laje. Contour across the steep slope, passing along the base of a cliff, turning a rocky corner where there may be a small waterfall. Later, the path runs along the base of another cliff, where there is a breach in the rock and steps zig-zag upwards. Later, while turning a rocky corner, there may be a view of the valley, though it is often cloudy during the day on this side of the mountains. Keep following the path as it rises and falls or uses mossy and uneven steps.

The zig-zag descent is obvious when it starts, and the path is less overgrown. There are occasional views down the valley to the sea, but there are also huge tils along the way and the woods can be quite dense. You are drawn along a path that has been cut down across a cliff face, but there is a rocky parapet so it does not feel exposed. There are twin **pinnacles** just below, and mossy, rocky steps lead down to a rocky cleft in the ridge. The path

Transport:
Camacha Bus 81 serves Colmeal. São Roque Bus 103 passes the Bar Fronteira near Boaventura. Rodoeste Bus 6 also serves Boaventura.

Refreshments:
There is a small bar at the head of the Curral valley. The Bar Fronteira is reached at the end of the walk near Boaventura.

turns around the roots of a big til in this cleft and continues down more steps. Zig-zag down through the undergrowth among tall tils and pass a shallow cave, then follow a terrace path cut from the slope. There are a few steps where the path passes through a small rocky gap, but before crossing, take a look back at the twin pinnacles. There is a glimpse of a road-end far below, though you will wonder how to reach it!

Keep following the path as it zig-zags further downhill. Sometimes it is stony underfoot, but it can be quite gentle and even too. At times the path is in a deeply worn groove, and although there are short-cuts through the zig-zags, it is best to stay on the main path for the easiest descent. Do not risk losing the way in the dense woods on this slope. The path is more uneven in an area of tall pines, brambles and rampant undergrowth, then continues down through tree heather and laurels. At a small gateway, some walkers cut a corner and follow a rocky path steeply downhill. Going through the gate, the path is easier, and swings round to come through another gate at a lower level. The rocky, grooved path has a few wooden steps, then it lands beside a **levada**. There is a path alongside the levada, but do not follow it. If you wonder where the water is going, it flows through some of the longest tunnels in Madeira to emerge as the Levada dos Tornos along the southern flanks of the island. (See Walk 1 and Walk 2.)

Continue down a path from the levada, which is narrow and stony at first, but becomes a broad paved path later. Pass willows before reaching the first house at **Lombo do Urzal**. Big concrete steps lead down past other houses and cross a concrete bridge over the bouldery **Ribeira do Porco**. Pause to look around the densely wooded mountains enclosing the valley, then continue down what appears to be a concrete road, though it ends with another flight of big steps. Land on a tarmac road at a turning space.

Follow the road uphill from Lombo do Urzal and pass a road junction to continue down through the valley. You will realise how remote Lombo do Urzal was before the road was built. Note the steep cultivation terraces and red-roofed storage sheds. There are plenty of vine trellises and the courses of levadas can be picked out. Turn right at a road junction to pass **Falca de Baixo** and its church. The road drops between a cliff and the river, and while crossing a bridge at the bottom, note the huge boulders in the riverbed. The road reaches a junction with a bend on the ER-101 road, and the **Bar Fronteira** is just to the right. There are buses along this road, though if there is time it is possible to walk to the nearby village of **Boaventura**.

WALK 21: Boca da Corrida to Fontes

THE ROUTE
Distance:
7.5km (4½ miles).
Start:
On the Boca da Corrida above Corticeiras – 142206.
Finish:
At the Bar Fontes at Fontes – 109197.
Maps:
Military Survey 1:25,000 Sheet 5 or IGC 1:50,000 Madeira West.
Terrain:
Mostly along easy tracks on open slopes, but the ascent of Terreiros involves crossing rough and stony slopes.

It is possible to use a bus to reach Corticeiras, then walk up the road to the **Boca da Corrida**, but it is a steep road. Refer to Walk 15 for details. A taxi can be hired near the church at Estreito de Câmara de Lobos to reach the high gap more quickly. The last part of the road is cobbled and leads to a small car park at the Posto Florestal Jardim da Serra around 1220m (4000ft). There are picnic tables and

Starting from the Boca da Corrida on a high gap around 1220m (4000ft), follow an easy track across a rugged slope, then head for the summit of Terreiros at 1436m (4711ft). After enjoying good views of the mountains for relatively little effort, descend to a good track and enjoy more good views on the way downhill. There is a particularly striking view of Serra de Água from the Crista do Espigão. A good track leads down to a road in the quiet little village of Fontes, where you can call for a taxi to get down to Ribeira Brava after the walk.

a shrine to São Cristovão in the shade of a few trees. Splendid views take in mountains from Pico Grande to Pico Ruivo and Pico do Areeiro, while Curral das Freiras lies deep in the valley.

Follow a track uphill through chained pillars, then left to climb up and across a slope covered in broom and brambles. The track turns right and zig-zags up and across the slope. Pass through an area of chestnuts and watch for little water-holes beside the track, made for sheep that graze these dry slopes. Keep walking to reach a junction of tracks. Take the track on the right, rising to an isolated white building close to a ridge leading to Terreiros. Walk above the building to link vague sheep paths leading to the ridge. Broom on this slope has been burnt, but will regenerate in time. Bear left to follow the rugged ridge, crossing a gap and following a fence uphill. There is a short, steep, rocky stretch, then short grass and bracken on the higher parts. Cross a fence junction using a crude stile, then follow a path beside the fence to reach the summit of **Terreiros** at 1436m (4711ft). Views stretch from the sea to the plateau of Paúl da Serra, then along the rugged mountain crest of Madeira and down towards Funchal.

Cross the fence on the summit and walk down a narrow path. Swing right across a gentle grassy slope to follow a grassy track gently downhill. The track winds on the slope and goes through a gateway, then there is a broad zig-zag on grass or stones before another gateway.

Transport:
Taxi to the Boca da Corrida. Taxi away from Fontes.

Refreshments:
The Bar Fontes is at Fontes at the end of the walk.

Goats may be tethered for grazing on the track down to Fontes

Reach a junction with another track, where there is a cutting with peculiar little cubbyholes alongside. Turn right here to follow the other broad track. The track runs gently down and around the head of a valley. Note a water-hole down to the left, for grazing animals. There is a gap in the ridge of **Crista do Espigão**, where there is a view across a deep, steep-sided valley to the lofty Pico Grande. Much the same view is gained from the next gap. When the track zig-zags downhill, there is a water-hole to the right and a view over a precipitous drop to Serra de Água.

The track wriggles away from the edge and drops down into an empty valley, descending to cross a streambed in an area of chestnut and eucalyptus. Emerge from the trees and there are old cultivation terraces and signs of former occupation. Continue down the stony track, and tangles of broom and brambles give way to cultivation terraces and small buildings. The track is rough and stony in places, but always clear to follow. Pass more chestnut and eucalyptus, then all of a sudden there are little houses and farms. A concrete road leads down to a tarmac road and the Bar Fontes in the little village of **Fontes** where the walk ends.

WALK 22: Fontes and Terreiros

THE ROUTE
Distance:
10km (6 miles).
Start/Finish:
At the Bar Fontes at Fontes – 109197.
Maps:
Military Survey 1:25,000 Sheet 5 or IGC 1:50,000 Madeira West.
Terrain:
Good tracks and paths throughout, on wooded and open slopes.

The Bar Fontes is in the little village of **Fontes** at an altitude of 936m (3071ft). Follow the road signposted for Campanário, gently downhill, around a valley and up past the Bar O Castanheiro, where there are a few chestnut trees. The road climbs and passes a few houses, then there is a slight descent and a bend to the right. Watch for a track rising sharply left, almost immediately swinging right.

The track is horribly dusty, except when it is very wet, in which case it is horribly muddy. It climbs among chestnuts, though these quickly give way to eucalyptus. Avoid turnings to left and right while following the track uphill. More chestnuts are reached at a higher level. Turn a bend where there is a view of the Campanário valley and the shapeless form of Terreiros at its head. The track climbs past the **Posto Florestal** Trompica, and continues ever upwards through eucalyptus. Pass through a gateway and eventually reach a more open slope dotted with chestnuts and covered in broom. Cattle, sheep and goats graze on this slope. Follow the winding track up through two more gateways to reach a track junction where a cutting has peculiar little cubbyholes alongside.

Swing sharply right at the junction to climb Terreiros, though you could omit the summit and stick to the main circuit. The spur track leads through a gateway and climbs gently. There is a broad zig-zag on short grass or stones, then another gateway. The grassy track gradually winds uphill until it is within sight of the rounded summit of **Terreiros**. At that point, head off to the right along a narrow path to reach the summit at a junction of a wall and fence at 1436m (4711ft). Views stretch from the sea to the plateau of Paúl da Serra, then along the rugged mountain crest of Madeira and down towards Funchal. Retrace steps down the narrow path and grassy track to reach the track junction.

Turn right to continue along the track, which runs gently down and around the head of a valley. Note a water-hole down to the left, for grazing animals. There is a gap in the ridge of **Crista do Espigão**, where there is a view across a deep, steep-sided valley to the lofty Pico Grande. Much the same view is gained from the next gap.

Get a taxi high up above Ribeira Brava to Fontes, to complete a fairly easy circuit along good tracks. Climb up a well-wooded slope, emerging with good views of the surrounding countryside. Improve the vista by taking a spur track and path to the summit of Terreiros at 1436m (4711ft). However, even staying on the main circuit, there are fine views through gaps along the Crista do Espigão and across Serra de Água to Paul da Serra. Tracks can be rather dusty at the start and you will choke if a truck comes past. After heavy rain they are very muddy.

Transport:
Taxi to and from Fontes.

Refreshments:
The Bar Fontes and Bar O Castanheiro are at the start.

111

When the track zig-zags downhill, there is a water-hole to the right and a view over a precipitous drop to Serra de Água.

The track wriggles away from the edge and drops down into an empty valley, descending to cross a streambed in an area of chestnut and eucalyptus. Emerge from the trees and there are old cultivation terraces and signs of former occupation. Continue down the stony track, and tangles of broom and brambles give way to cultivation terraces and small buildings. The track is rough and stony in places, but is always clear to follow. Pass more chestnut and eucalyptus, then all of a sudden there are little houses and farms. A concrete road leads down to a tarmac road, back at the Bar **Fontes** where the walk started.

WALK 23: Levada do Norte – part 1

The Levada do Norte measures 38km (21½ miles) and can be divided into two remarkably different stretches. The first, from Estreito de Câmara de Lobos to Boa Morte, is fairly easy and popular. The continuation from Boa Morte to Serra de Água is horribly exposed in places and consequently less popular. Taking the easy stretch first, enjoy following the levada across well-cultivated and well-settled slopes, passing by Garachico, Quinta Grande and Campanário. The levada runs at a general altitude of 550m (1805ft).

THE ROUTE

Distance:
18km (11 miles).

Start:
On the levada above Estreito de Câmara de Lobos – 146167.

Finish:
At the Snack Bar O Coelho at Boa Morte – 087174.

Maps:
Military Survey 1:25,000 Sheet 8 or IGC 1:50,000 Madeira West.

Terrain:
The levada path is level and either crosses well-cultivated slopes or goes through wooded valleys. Some short stretches are exposed.

Start where the bus to Corticeiras crosses the Levada do Norte above Estreito de Câmara de Lobos. If the bus terminates at the church at **Estreito**, then climb a steep road with the Stations of the Cross alongside to reach the levada. A large sign on the left indicates where the levada runs across a slope of vine trellises, and this is useful as the channel is covered with concrete slabs. Follow the paved path round into a little valley, then the water is seen and can be followed upstream. Later, the channel is paved and crosses two concrete roads close together before it is open again. Walk round into another little valley and the channel is alternately open and covered. Pass houses and vines, as well as fruit and vegetable plots, then the houses end on the way into a larger valley.

The levada path narrows and there are ominous overhanging rocks, but do not worry. Go down a few steps and along a lower path, then up a few steps to continue. The levada path narrows again, so be careful of overhanging rock. An easier path continues to the wild and wooded head of the valley, where there are two concrete footbridges; the latter over the Ribeira da Caixa. There is a rock wall beside the levada, then continue through mixed woods. There are views stretching from the sea up the valley to Corticeiras. Moving out of the valley, part of Funchal is seen beyond the church at Estreito de Câmara de Lobos.

Pass under overhanging rock while swinging out of the valley to overlook the hilltop church at **Garachico**. The levada is covered in slabs as it passes houses, then steps lead up to a road. A painted sign advises that there is a bar 700m (765yds) uphill, otherwise walk down the road a few paces and use steps to get back onto the levada. The channel is still covered in slabs and flanked by agapanthus, passing a spur where tall pines grow. Swing round into the next valley, then there are plenty of houses along the way. The levada is again covered by slabs and has street lights alongside. A house covers the channel, so walk down steps, then back uphill to continue. The levada is covered in slabs and there is a landslip ahead, where a building collapsed and tore a section of the channel away. The water flows through a buried pipe, so pick a way down a slope of mimosa bushes, then head back uphill to continue along the next

Transport:
Rodoeste Bus 96 crosses the levada at Estreito de Câmara de Lobos. Rodoeste Bus 127 and 148 serve Boa Morte.

Refreshments:
There are bars at Estreito de Câmara de Lobos, Cabo Girão and Boa Morte.

The hilltop church at Garachico seen from the Levada do Norte

covered stretch. The levada crosses the ER-229 road, so go down a few steps to continue along the covered channel. The water is seen again as it turns tightly round a valley above **Caldeira**, then it turns a corner and cuts across a steep slope. Agapanthus and brambles grow beside the levada, with prickly pears on some parts. Rocky stretches have a fence alongside, so there is less exposure. A sudden swing to the right leads though a short tunnel with an uneven path at Cabo Girão. Above the tunnel are the main road, bus stop and a bar.

Leave the tunnel and turn right to enter the valley of **Quinta Grande**. The channel is covered for a stretch, then open again as it turns round the head of the valley. The main road is just above the levada. Climb up to it at a road bridge. Turn left down the road and look out for a sign reading 'Levada do Norte' on the right. The channel is covered, then open, running just above the road. It passes houses and runs between eucalyptus and pines on a curved stretch. There is a fence alongside at a rock cutting, then it crosses a steep and cobbled track. Another stretch has fencing alongside, as well as bamboo and brambles, then there are pines and eucalyptus on a slope above. Swing out of the valley and follow concrete walkways, crossing a couple of concrete roads close together. Walk between tall fences to pass a sluice system. Walk among shady chestnuts and mimosa, as well as crossing a slope of tall pines. Houses stand below the levada on the way round into the Campanário valley.

Pass tall pines and eucalyptus while walking round a small side valley, with views down to the church and houses at **Campanário**. There is a short fenced stretch, then cross cultivation terraces full of fruit and vegetables, including apples. The levada loops across a well-wooded slope, passing tall eucalyptus and pines as it aims for the head of the valley. Cross a levada stepping stone footbridge over the **Ribeira do Campanário**. Eucalyptus gives way to pine while swinging into another valley head, and chestnut and mimosa are passed before there is a tight turn to leave the valley. Mimosa and pine give way to cultivated slopes and a house, then the levada has street lights alongside. Pass terraces covered in fruit and vegetables, and a few more houses, then cross a concrete road at a water intake and swing sharply round into a side valley. The path is lined with agapanthus above a sports pitch. Pass chestnuts and a circular reservoir, then pass tall pines while turning round the head of the valley. Cross a tarmac road on the other side of the sports pitch and continue along the levada.

There are a couple of tucks in the valley side, and a couple of houses are passed, then the levada crosses a slope dotted with a few chestnuts. There is one house beside the levada, then some tall pines. The path is nicely planted with flowers and shrubs as it passes another house. Leave the levada and follow a track down to a road and the Snack Bar O Pinheiro. Take a break here, or if catching a bus, continue down the road through **Boa Morte** to the Snack Bar O Coelho. To walk along the more exposed part of the Levada do Norte, refer to Walk 24.

WALK 24: Levada do Norte – part 2

The Levada do Norte is simple and straightforward between Estreito de Câmara de Lobos and Boa Morte. Its character changes beyond Boa Morte. The route is quiet and well wooded, with a big loop round a valley at Ribeira Funda. After that the levada becomes more and more exposed, picking its way across steep slopes and sheer cliffs, as well as passing through ten tunnels. A section of the levada collapsed in the year 2000 and was replaced by piping. Check that this has been repaired before attempting the walk. A wide loop and a long tunnel above Serra de Água takes the levada to the Serra de Água generating station.

THE ROUTE

Distance:
17km (10½ miles).

Start:
At the Snack Bar O Coelho at Boa Morte – 087174.

Finish:
At the Pousada dos Vinháticos above Serra de Água – 105235.

Maps:
Military Survey 1:25,000 Sheets 5 and 8 or IGC 1:50,000 Madeira West.

Terrain:
The levada path is initially easy, crossing wooded or cultivated slopes, but later it is very exposed on cliff faces and goes through ten tunnels.

Start in **Boa Morte** and walk up the road from the Snack Bar O Coelho to the Snack Bar O Pinheiro. Continue a little further up the road to see the Levada do Norte is signposted to the right for Quinta Grande and to the left for Serra de Água. Turn left to follow it upstream, where it is attractively lined with agapanthus and loops through tall pines that suffered a burning in the past. There is more eucalyptus among the pines, then there is a view through the valley from the Boca da Encumeada to Ribeira Brava. Follow the levada round a corner, across a slope of eucalyptus, into a side valley. Wild and mixed woods are passed while crossing a footbridge at the head of this valley, then there are a few houses at **Ribeira Funda** and cultivation terraces. Leave the side valley and note the little settlement of Eira do Mourado perched on a knoll below the levada.

The slope above the levada is rocky in places, but not excessively, and the slope below is steep in places, but not vertical. The path is narrow and grassy, with gentle loops, and looking down into the valley there is a view of the large Modela supermarket. Further along, the slope is much steeper and the path is narrow and uneven, needing greater care. Cross shrubby cliffs, then turn round a corner, through a small rock cutting, to reach a side valley. Chestnuts grow here, and there is a small **tunnel** and caves, followed by more chestnuts and less exposure. Swing round the head of the valley, which is drained by the Ribeira do Espigão, and alternately cross exposed and wooded stretches. There is an overhanging part where wet grass drips onto the path, and it could be slippery. Reach a fern-covered **tunnel** entrance, where a torch is needed to get through, and bear in mind that the path can be muddy and wet. There is a wall between the path and the channel, and good headroom. It is rather exposed at the exit from the tunnel, with a view to the Boca da Encumeada. The path is flanked by agapanthus. Watch out for overhanging rock. The path is less exposed as it passes more chestnuts. Some short stretches of the channel are covered and there is an awkward and rather exposed overhang, then turn round a rocky corner where there is a short rock cutting. Turn another corner and go through another small cutting, then walk round a rather tight gully, followed by a smaller gully. There are several short exposed stretches afterwards, with occasional agapanthus, candleberry or the odd rock for scant security. Cut across a sheer cliff that is very exposed, and there is a shower of drips at the end where the channel is covered. Slippery steps lead down into another **tunnel**. There is good headroom and a wall between the path and channel, but it is curved, so the exit is not immediately in view.

Emerge on an even more exposed stretch, where the cliff face peeled away and took the levada with it in the year 2000. A repair was effected with lengths of piping, so check in advance if this has been consolidated. (Maybe use binoculars and examine the rock face from the main road a short way below the Snack Bar Serra de

Transport:
Rodoeste Bus 127 and 148 serve Boa Morte. Rodoeste Bus 6 and 139 serve the Pousada dos Vinháticos above Serra de Água.

Refreshments:
The Snack Bar O Coelho and Snack Bar O Pinheiro are at Boa Morte. The Pousada dos Vinháticos is reached at the end of the walk.

Água.) There is another short and curved **tunnel**, with a wall between the path and the channel, and the path can be very muddy. On leaving the tunnel it is very exposed. Beware of rockfalls, then turn round a corner and pass more chestnuts. The next short **tunnel** has a muddy path and low headroom. Exit with trees alongside, so it does not feel too exposed, but there is also overhanging rock, so watch your head. Turn round another corner and look up to spot a tower of rock. The path is fairly bushy and secure as it swings round the base of the tower, then there is yet another **tunnel**. This one has low headroom, a wall between the path and the channel, and the path is wet and muddy. Emerge in a shady area of mixed woodland and continue along the levada. Agapanthus grows where there is enough soil for a path, otherwise walk along the parapet. Chestnut, laurel and heather grow in places, and there are views of high mountains while swinging round into a big valley drained by the Ribeiro do Pico.

The path is very exposed while turning round a cliff and there are fine mountain views. There is a wooded patch, then overhanging rock and another exposed corner below Pico Frade. Agapanthus grows beside the path and there are dense chestnut woods. Emerging from the woods, the levada flows through a curious concrete sluice system, where some water is drawn off and fed through a tunnel to Curral das Freiras. Climb and descend short flights of steps while crossing the valley to find the levada and path continuing upstream.

Cross a steep slope, which is well wooded and there is no sense of exposure. Pass through a cutting where the channel is covered and there is a big stump of rock to the left. There is also a striking view of the Pico do Búzio ahead. There are wooded and exposed stretches, then a sudden right turn through a short **tunnel** under the little Pico do Meio-Vintém. There is low headroom, so be careful. A mixture of trees and shrubs fill a side valley and it is not too exposed while walking to its bouldery head. There is a long **tunnel**; in fact this is the longest of the ten tunnels on the walk, over 1km ($\frac{1}{2}$ mile) in length. At first there is low headroom, but things improve further along, and the path is wide, but uneven. There are not

The view from a tunnel of Serra de Água and the Boca de Encumeada

too many drips or puddles. Watch out for sloping stretches of path, as well as occasional low headroom, and the path seems to narrow towards the end. Emerge and cross a levada stepping stone footbridge across the Ribeiro do **Poço**.

The path is a bit exposed as it cuts across the valley side, but it is also fairly well wooded and shrubby too. Beware of loose landslip debris covering the levada. The path leads to a short **tunnel**, where there are steps down to enter and steps up to leave. There is a good path and good headroom. Emerge in a green gully surmounted by a huge wedged boulder and immediately enter the final short **tunnel**. Take care here, as the rock is a bouldery agglomerate and some pieces are loose. Agapanthus lines the path and there is a good mixture of trees, as well as street lighting alongside the levada. There is an awkward overhang while working into a valley, then climb up steps and walk round a fenced parapet on the side of the **Central de Serra de Água** generating station. The end of the walk is simple; just follow the concrete access road away from the buildings. This crosses over a gentle rise on a wooded slope, then runs downhill and uphill, reaching the ER-104 road at the **Pousada dos Vinháticos** above Serra de Água.

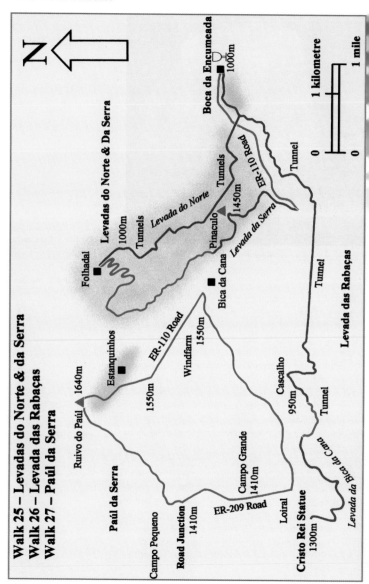

Walk 25 – Levadas do Norte & da Serra
Walk 26 – Levada das Rabaças
Walk 27 – Paúl da Serra

WALK 25: Levadas do Norte and da Serra

THE ROUTE
Distance:
18km (11 miles).
Start/Finish:
Boca da Encumeada – 112255.
Maps:
Military Survey 1:25,000 Sheet 5 or IGC 1:50,000 Madeira West.
Terrain:
Although the two levadas are level, they are quite difficult. The lower levada has a series of tunnels. A track and rugged, densely wooded mountain path lead to the higher levada. The descent is steep and rocky.

Start at the **Boca da Encumeada** beside the Snack Bar Restaurante Encumeada. Just across the road a couple of flights of steps lead up to the Levada do Norte and a sign points left upstream for Folhadal. The path is easy at first, and though well wooded, there are breaks along the way. Agapanthus flanks the levada and there are conifers, oak, laurel, heather and malfurada. Walk past a house and enjoy easy loops. There is a view back to the pass from an overhanging rock cutting. Pico Grande and other mountains can be seen across the deeply-cut valley. When a **tunnel** is seen to the right, reach for a torch. There is low headroom at the start, but the path is good. Later, there is more space to manoeuvre and plenty of headroom, but the path is uneven. There are drips in the middle. Exit onto a good path flanked by agapanthus and hydrangea. The steep slopes are covered in ancient, dense 'laurisilva' woodland, with moist air supporting mosses and ferns. The path is fenced in places, looping gently round the slope, with little sense of exposure and a few views between the trees.

Two remarkably different levadas can be linked on the steep and wooded north-eastern escarpment of Paúl da Serra. Start from the Boca da Encumeada and follow the Levada do Norte through six tunnels. The altitude is 1000m (3280ft). The levada continues through even more tunnels, but this route heads uphill on a zig-zag track and well-wooded path to reach a higher levada. The Levada da Serra slices across a cliff face at 1450m (4760ft) and is quite exciting. A rough, rocky, zig-zag path drops down to the ER-110, which runs through three tunnels to return to the Boca da Encumeada.

A big stump of rock called Pinaculo seen from the Levada do Serra

Walk though a short **tunnel**, then there is a slender waterfall off to the left and the surroundings are very green, moist and jungly. Ahead is another **tunnel** entrance, whose mouth is rich with mosses. There is low headroom on entering, and it is rather narrow, with an uneven path. There is more room later, with a better path, though it remains rather narrow. The levada is deep and wide, so do not fall into it! It is usually wet at the exit, and the levada is covered in stone slabs. There is tree heather, laurel and malfurada along the next few easy loops, and the levada is covered in places.

The next **tunnel** has low entrance, with a narrow path, though the path is mostly even and there is more room in the middle. It narrows again towards the exit, then cross a well-wooded gully with a little waterfall to the left. Almost immediately, walk into another **tunnel**. There is mostly good headroom, and the path is even, but some parts are a bit narrow. Emerge on a wooded slope, then walk a short way and enter yet another **tunnel**, which is quite short and easy. There are views between the trees on the next steep slope, and although the path is unfenced, there is little feeling of exposure. The levada has been cut from a rocky slope and there is an over-hang. An easy stretch loops round the slope and reaches a levada keeper's cottage at **Folhadal**. There is another house further along, but do not walk that far.

Follow a broad and stony track uphill from the levada. There are views into the valley and down to the sea while climbing. The track rises in easy zig-zags and is flanked by deep heather and brambles, with a few laurels and sometimes an extensive ground cover of lichens, as well as plenty of bracken. There is an old levada channel off to the left on one of the bends, then the track has some rough and stony stretches and rises past a crumbling cutting with some large specimens of tree heather on top. Watch carefully to spot a path heading off to the left at a bend, where there may be arrows scratched onto boulders to point the way. Step down from the track, then walk up and along the narrow path through dense 'laurisilva' woodland. There is tall tree heather, laurel, tall bilberry and a ground cover of bracken. The path climbs gradually and is mossy and stony, but fairly clear despite being narrow. There are some level stretches and a couple of fallen trees, as well as a short bouldery stretch. Keep climbing and traverse across the foot of a series of cliffs, which may be dripping in places. The path is usually good, but may be very narrow where it runs through bracken, heather and bilberry, and if there is a crumbling earth edge, then take care. Enjoy a view of Madeira's highest peaks from time to time. (If time is short and an exit is needed, note that a path marked with a blue symbol leads up to the ER-110 road at **Bica da Cana**.)

Transport:
Rodoeste Bus 6 and 139 serve the Boca da Encumeada.

Refreshments:
The Snack Bar Restaurante Encumeada is at the start/finish.

Keeping to the path, pass through tall bilberry, cross muddy patches, walk through heather and traverse along the foot of dripping cliffs. Take all this in your stride and enjoy the views. Look ahead to spot the line of the **Levada da Serra.** Turn round a steep-sided hollow in the mountainside to find the narrow levada channel. Little streams and the drips from the cliff are collected and flow downstream. The path is often narrow and flanked by dense heather. Pass a sign reading 'Casa de Abrigo do Caramujo'. There are some steep drops, but little sense of exposure because of the vegetation. Take care where the levada path is broken, usually because of rockfalls from the sheer cliff above. The path becomes easier and there is a wide stance where a break can be taken beside the big stump of rock called Pináculo. Again there is a view of the highest peaks on Madeira.

The levada suddenly runs down a steep chute. Do not follow it, but look for stone steps nearby to descend. The flow remains vigorous and an easy path is marked with occasional plane trees, though it is mostly tall tree heather growing across the slope. There are a couple more steep chutes while turning a corner, then a splendid view of peaks and valleys beyond Encumeada. The road is far below and you may wonder how to reach it. Follow a narrow, well-trodden path well to the left of the levada chute. Start zig-zagging down a steep and rocky slope covered in broom and heather, crossing the levada chute twice. A terrace path and flight of steps leads along and down a cliff into tree heather. There is wonderfully mixed vegetation while crossing the levada again, now seen as a lovely little waterfall. Walk alongside the channel again using a good path through dense vegetation. Cross a drippy, slippery rock lip and continue past weeping walls, then the water runs through a pipe. Take care when stepping onto a blind bend on the **ER-110 road**. Turn left to follow the road downhill. It leads through three **tunnels** to return to the **Boca da Encumeada.**

WALK 26: Cascalho and Levada das Rabaças

THE ROUTE

Distance:

12km (7½ miles).

Start:

On the ER-209 road below the Cristo Rei statue –
034241.

Finish:

Boca da Encumeada – 112255.

Maps:

Military Survey 1:25,000 Sheet 5 or IGC 1:50,000
Madeira West.

Terrain:

Rugged in places. The levada is easy at the start, then
there is a stony track down to Cascalho. The levada
leading onwards is more exposed and goes through a
long tunnel to reach the Boca da Encumeada.

Start below the **Cristo Rei statue** high on the ER-209 road,
where the Levada do Paúl crosses the road at an altitude
of 1300m (4265ft). Pass in front of a building and walk
through a small cutting, passing a twin feeder channel.
Follow the **Levada da Bica da Cana** upstream through
deep heather and broom and swing into a little valley.
Cross a slope of bracken and pass a curious chimney and
pine tree. Cross a cobbled road and walk up an incline.
Cross a gentle gap on a ridge, go through a gate and turn
left into a bigger valley.

The levada path leads in easy loops across a steep
and rugged slope, looking down on the parallel course
of the Levada Seca. There is an exposed concrete parapet,
then be careful of rock leaning over the channel. The path
continues as a grassy, stony or earthen line, with a few
short exposed parts, crossing a steep slope covered in
heather. Turn right down a broad track, pass a cave carved

Cascalho is an
amazingly rugged
valley head, where
water pours down
rocky gullies, weeps
and trickles from sheer
cliffs and oozes from
sodden slopes of
vegetation. Small
wonder that levadas
have been carved
around the valley and
tunnels bored through
the mountains to
channel the water
away. This walk follows
the gentle Levada da
Bica da Cana into the
valley, then uses a
stony track to drop
down onto the more
exposed Levada das
Rabaças. The longest
levada tunnel in this
guidebook comes next,
measuring about 2.3km
(1½ miles). There are
more short exposed
stretches and another
tunnel then an easier
stretch leads to the
Boca da Encumeada.

Transport:
Nova minibuses visit
Paúl da Serra, otherwise
use a taxi. Rodoeste Bus
6 and 139 serve the
Boca da Encumeada.

Refreshments:
The Snack Bar
Restaurante Encumeada
is at the end of the walk.

in the pumice bedrock, and descend in loops across the steep mountainside. The track passes a derelict building where there are fine views of the rugged valley head at Cascalho. There is a **tunnel** with an impressive amount of headroom, but it is curved and the exit is not immediately seen. There is also a levada flowing across the floor so use a torch. Take care as the rock is bouldery and chunks fall down from time to time.

Walk down from the tunnel to find a couple more tunnels in the cliff to the left. Both tunnels are blocked so do not enter them. Instead, follow the **Levada das Rabaças** downstream on an inclined channel. Walk with care as it is a bit exposed and there is a fence alongside. Follow the levada to the head of the rock-walled amphitheatre at **Cascalho**, and cross a stack of boulders. Spend a while marvelling at the waterfalls around the valley; some of them gushing and others falling as misty curtains. The levada path is narrow and exposed in places, but mostly fenced as it proceeds from the head of the valley. Take care when there is no fence, and turn round the mountainside. The levada loops across the steep and rugged slope with fencing alongside, and works its way round another rock-walled amphitheatre. There are only a few tall trees and plenty of heather. The Ribeira da Ponta do Sol drains the valley, but at the point where it is reached, you are drawn into a tunnel.

This **tunnel** takes an hour or so to negotiate. A torch and spare batteries are necessary. The roof is low at the entrance and the path is uneven, but there is more room and the path is better further inside. There is a wall between the path and the channel for a while then one stretch of the tunnel is lined with concrete. The path becomes patchy for a while and there comes a point where the tunnel mouths are mere pinpricks of light. Persevere. The path may slope towards the channel or be slippery, then it becomes drier and firmer. Cross a concrete hump where the path drops, and there is a wall between the path and the channel again. The path is wet and muddy, and headroom limited for a while, but things get better closer to the exit. The path improves before emerging into daylight.

Turn left on leaving the tunnel to pass fine waterfalls. There is an isolated building above the levada, but keep an eye on the exposed and unprotected path. There are fine views across the valley to Pico Grande. Some parts are fenced and there is a stand of trees at the mouth of another **tunnel**. This tunnel is not too long, but still requires a torch. It goes beneath Pico das Furnas and is rather drippy at both ends, with puddles most of the way. However, the path is generally wide, with a wall between it and the channel, and there is good headroom. There are a few trees near the exit, as well as a bouldery streambed.

Be careful of overhanging rock further along the levada. The channel is covered in a number of places against rockfall and landslip debris. Pass a huge boulder sitting over the levada and go through a small gateway. Short stretches of the levada are covered as it continues in loops across the steep mountainside, and there are good views across the valley to the mountains beyond. There is more tree cover as along a stony path. Pass a rectangular impound, then continue along a narrow concrete parapet. Note a tunnel off to the left. Do not go through it, but bear it in mind for another day and refer to Walk 25 for a route in that direction. Pass an over-hanging rock cutting where there is a view ahead to the Boca da Encumeada, and easy loops lead past a house to reach the gap. There is a fine mixture of trees and shrubs along the way, including conifers, oak, laurel, heather and malfurada. Agapanthus grows alongside the path. Go down a flight of steps and cross the road to reach the Snack Bar Restaurante **Encumeada.**

WALK 27: Paúl da Serra

Paúl da Serra is a broad, bracken-covered plateau around 1400–1600m (4600–5250ft), sloping gently uphill from west to east. It has the appearance of a bleak, rolling moorland enclosed by rounded little hills. Roads cross it in all directions and there is quite a network of paths and tracks. When cloud builds up around Madeira, it laps against the plateau edges, then suddenly rolls over and covers everything. To walk on Paúl da Serra, pick a sunny day and start early. On a windy day, you will realise why the plateau edges were planted with wind turbines! The walk takes in the broad central area, as well as the highest point on the plateau, which is Ruivo do Paúl at 1640m (5380ft).

The Route

Distance:
13km (8 miles).

Start/Finish:
At a corner on the ER-110 road on Paúl da Serra – 037262.

Maps:
Military Survey 1:25,000 Sheet 5 or IGC 1:50,000 Madeira West.

Terrain:
Gently sloping moorland covered in bracken. Paths and tracks can be vague or stony underfoot. Care is needed with route-finding in mist.

Start on a corner of the ER-110 road high on Paúl da Serra, at a **road junction** with a broad dirt road. The altitude is 1410m (4625ft). The dirt road is signposted for Fanal and Ribeira da Janela, and the main road is signposted for Rabaçal, Canhas and distant Funchal. Follow the dirt road, swinging right and left to cross a bouldery, ochreous streambed. Walk further, noting the slight embankment to the right. Turn right to go through a breach in the embankment and follow a less distinct grassy track. Note the short-cropped grass and liberal scattering of stones. The track reaches the left-hand corner of a tall fenced enclosure. Swing right round the corner, then left to rise gently up a slope of bracken. There is a very vague line used by wheeled vehicles, rising gently with bracken to the left and ochreous boulders to the right. There is a stony streak, then walk with bracken to the left and notice that stones have been pushed to the right, leaving the surface mostly grassy. Ahead, a patch of forest forms the skyline, with a rounded, bracken-covered hill to the left. The hill is Ruivo do Paúl.

A clear, stony, grassy track rises easily through the bracken towards the hill and the forest. After a very slight descent, reach a point where a clearer grassy track slices in from right to left. Turn left to follow it, swinging well to the left of the forest, then intersect with another track. Turn right to walk towards the forest, but do not enter it. Instead, turn left and rise up narrow, grassy paths through the bracken to climb to the summit of **Ruivo do Paúl**. There is a trig point at 1640m (5380ft). There are fine views around the Paúl da Serra plateau. Madeira's highest peaks are in view too, and sometimes there is an ocean of level cloud.

Turn right to follow a tall fence downhill. Use a patchy path on a grass and bracken slope that is stony in places, to reach a track junction down on a gap. Turn right down the grassy track, following it through bracken as it becomes stonier and is flanked by gorse. Continue between young conifers to reach a junction with another track. Turn left, gently uphill, and cross a tarmac road that serves **Estanquinhos**. Continue along the track, down and across a dip, with forest to the left and bracken and gorse to the right. The track runs into the main **ER-110 road**, so bear left to follow it onwards. There is no need to walk on the tarmac as there is plenty of space to the right of the road. Pass a sign explaining about the Parques Eólicos, or **windfarm**, and there are turbines to right and left of the road. Walk parallel to the road across a bouldery grassland, and watch how the road runs through a rock cutting to reach Bica da Cana. Spot a track beside the road and follow this until it is below an embankment beyond the cutting. Buildings are seen in the trees at **Bica da Cana**, but do not walk that far.

The track swings sharply right and runs downhill into a hollow of grass, bracken, gorse and broom. Follow it through a straggly fence and walk gently uphill. The track is roughly aligned to a fence as it crosses a rise, then it is stony as it descends into a shallow valley full of bracken. If it is too stony, then walk close to the fence on narrow paths through the bracken. The track crosses a stony riverbed, then is pleasant and grassy as it drifts away from the fence and through the bracken. Wind turbines whirl

Transport:
Nova minibuses visit Paúl da Serra, otherwise use a taxi.

Refreshments:
None. The nearest place is the Jungle Rain Café on the ER-110 in the direction of Porto Moniz.

Walkers admire an ocean of cloud from the summit of Ruivo do Paúl

on the brow to the right. Later the track is worn down to boulders and pumice bedrock, and is awkward to follow. When the track is blocked by boulders, continue straight onwards, or walk alongside if it is too rough, though it is easier later. The fence is again to the left, but drift away and reach a grassy track junction. Keep left and the grassy track becomes stonier, still running gently downhill, again with the fence to the left. At a junction, turn left along a clear track, still through bracken, with the fence alongside, and keep to the most obvious line as the track swings to the right and left and finally reaches the **ER-209 road**.

A sign by the road reads 'Paúl da Serra'. Turn right to follow the road, noting how a stone-built embankment supports the road and keeps it high above the broad moorland. Cross the little channel of the Levadinha da Serra and notice another stone embankment heading off to the right. There are wide views across the level grasslands of the **Campo Grande**, and you could leave the road and walk parallel for a while, though the ground can be wet after heavy rain. Come back onto the road at a well-signposted junction of the ER-209 and ER-110. Follow the road straight onwards, as signposted for Porto Moniz, to return to the **road junction** where the day's walk started.

WALK 28: Paúl da Serra to Fanal

THE ROUTE

Distance:
18km (11 miles) there and back.

Start/Finish:
At a corner on the ER-110 road on Paúl da Serra – 037262.

Maps:
Military Survey 1:25,000 Sheets 1, 4 and 5 or IGC 1:50,000 Madeira West.

Terrain:
A moorland track is broad, clear, easy and obvious throughout, later routed through tree heather and woodlands.

Start on a corner of the ER-110 road high on Paúl da Serra, at a **road junction** with a broad dirt road. The altitude is 1410m (4625ft). The dirt road is signposted for Fanal and Ribeira da Janela, and the main road is signposted for Rabaçal, Canhas and distant Funchal. Follow the dirt road, swinging right and left to cross a bouldery, ochreous streambed. Walk further, rising gently on a slope of grass and bracken. Cross a very gentle gap, then

For years there has been a plan to construct a road from Ribeira de Janela to Paúl da Serra, and in preparation, a substantial track was bulldozed to link both places. Since then, a winding tarmac road has been constructed up from Ribeira de Janela to Fanal, where there are some impressive and ancient til trees. The rest of the route may one day vanish under tarmac, but for the time being it is possible to walk from Paúl da Serra to Fanal and back without meeting more than a couple of vehicles. It is an easy high-level route, with some good views.

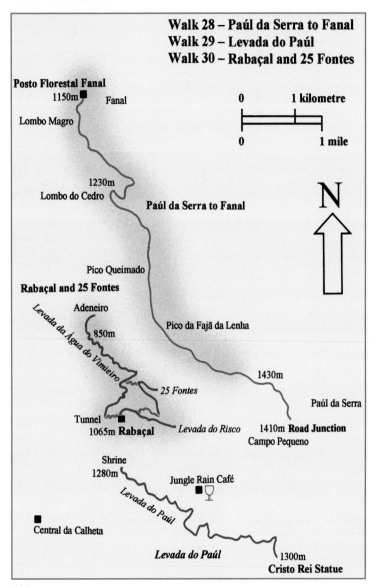

Walk 28 – Paúl da Serra to Fanal
Walk 29 – Levada do Paúl
Walk 30 – Rabaçal and 25 Fontes

Posto Florestal Fanal
1150m   Fanal

0   1 kilometre

0   1 mile

Lombo Magro

1230m
Lombo do Cedro

Paúl da Serra to Fanal

N

Pico Queimado

Rabaçal and 25 Fontes

Adeneiro

850m

Levada da Água do Vimieiro

Pico da Fajã da Lenha

25 Fontes

1430m

Tunnel   Rabaçal

1065m   *Levada do Risco*

Paúl da Serra

1410m **Road Junction**
Campo Pequeno

Shrine
1280m

Jungle Rain Café

Levada do Paúl

Central da Calheta

Levada do Paúl

1300m

Cristo Rei Statue

Afternoon cloud laps against the plateau edges on Paúl da Serra, Walk 27

on the descent fencing encloses the track, and there is dense heather cover. Occasionally there are views to the left of Rabaçal and its steep-sided, wooded valley. After crossing a cattle grid the track is unfenced.

Broom and laurel grow alongside the track, as well as tall bilberry, but these peter out and give way to heather for the most part. Views of Rabaçal recede and there is a glimpse of the high crest across the valley around Fonte do Bispo. The track levels out in a broad area around **Pico Queimado**. Continue the gentle descent through the heather. There are views either side as the crest narrows, and looking down to the right to Seixal takes in a particularly steep-sided valley.

There is a gentle ascent through a cutting excavated in the pumice bedrock. Pass some fine tils among the heather and bilberry. Drop downhill, swinging well to the right, then later well to the left in wide loops. The track levels out in an area that is mostly under heather cover. Rise slightly round a hillside where there is a big cutting in the pumice bedrock. There are also fine views down to the Janela valley. Swing round the hillside and continue downhill, passing some tall tils. At a track junction, turn right uphill to reach the **Posto Florestal Fanal**, where there are outstanding tall and ancient tils. Mosses,

Transport:
Nova minibuses visit Paúl da Serra, otherwise use a taxi.

Refreshments:
None. The nearest place is the Jungle Rain Café on the ER-110 in the direction of Porto Moniz.

lichens and ferns cling to the damp trunks, which are kept moist by the mists that roll over these slopes.

If you can arrange to be collected at Fanal, then the overall distance can be halved. Walking back to Paúl da Serra for a parked car, or to be collected there, means walking the full distance. As Fanal is at an altitude of 1200m (3940ft), remember that it is gently uphill most of the way back, and that it will take a little longer than the outward journey.

WALK 29: Levada do Paúl

The Levada do Paúl offers a short, easy, gentle walk along the south-western fringes of the Paúl da Serra plateau. Start on the main ER-110 road at the junction with the road leading down to Rabaçal, and end on the ER-209 road just below the prominent Cristo Rei statue and car park. If a car is used, then it is easy enough to walk both ways. Nova minibuses drop off walkers to walk the levada, collecting them later by arrangement. The walk can be extended, increasing the difficulty, by continuing along the levada for Cascalho, Rabaças and the Boca da Encumeada. For details refer to Walk 26.

THE ROUTE
Distance:
5km (3 miles).
Start:
On the ER-110 road at the junction with the Rabaçal road – 005257.
Finish:
On the ER-209 road below the Cristo Rei statue – 034241.
Maps:
Military Survey 1:25,000 Sheets 4 and 5 or IGC 1:50,000 Madeira West.
Terrain:
The levada path is mostly level and easy, but narrow and stony in places.

Start at the roadside car park where the Rabaçal road descends from the main ER-110 road on the western side of Paúl da Serra. The Levada do Paúl is found across the road and a little down a slope, to the left of a small **shrine**. Follow it upstream away from a big water tank. The levada is a small concrete channel slicing across a steep slope of grass, heather and bracken. At first, the road is only a short distance above the levada. Cross over a track that crosses the channel. As the ground becomes rockier, there are masses of gorse bushes, and the path is uneven as it passes a series of small caves. The path makes a tight loop across a small stream, which is at the head of the Ribeira do Pico da Urze. Although the path drifts from the road it is not far from the **Jungle Rain Café.**

The slope is covered in bracken while turning round a corner, then turn round another corner and cross another little stream. This is at the head of the Ribeira do Caldeirão. The slope continues to be covered in bracken, though as it becomes more rugged, it has a lot more broom and brambles. Later, while passing a cave, there is some tree heather and tall bilberry. The levada path swings round into another little valley to cross a streambed, then cuts across a slope of broom and bracken, reaching the ER-209 road at a green sign. There is a levada cottage across the road, and a short way up the road is the **Cristo Rei statue** and a car park.

Transport:
Nova minibuses visit Paúl da Serra and Rabaçal, or use a taxi.

Refreshments:
The Jungle Rain Café is fairly close to the levada.

A gnarled example of tree heather overhangs the levada

WALK 30: Rabaçal and 25 Fontes

Walking at Rabaçal is usually accomplished by those who have their own cars. A taxi could be hired, and minibuses also reach this wonderfully wooded enclave. The rugged valley head abounds with streams and springs, and these have been tapped by several levadas. Following them on a map is confusing, while following them on the ground leaves people wondering why they were made. Explore for long enough to find that water is channelled out of the valley, through a huge tunnel, to the distant Central da Calheta generating station. Use this route to walk along three levadas, and visit the intriguing 25 Fontes.

THE ROUTE

Distance:
13km (8 miles).

Start/Finish:
Rabaçal – 004265.

Maps:
Military Survey 1:25,000 Sheet 4 or
IGC 1:50,000 Madeira West.

Terrain:
The levada paths are level, but although some are broad, others are very narrow and sometimes exposed. There are also steep, rugged paths on well-wooded slopes leading between the levadas, as well as flights of steps.

Rabaçal is reached by a steep and winding dead-end road signposted downhill from the main ER-110 road on the western side of Paúl da Serra. There is a car park beside isolated houses at the wooded head of a valley. The altitude is 1065m (3495ft) and the walk drops down in stages before climbing back up later in the day. There are many paths, and many ways to link them together. It is also possible to bring the walk to a rapid end, but study a map to spot the options.

To start, simply follow a clear and stony track downhill from the houses, patched with concrete in places. It levels out and the **Levada do Risco** can be followed away to the right. Walk past a small sign at a path junction confirming that this is the Risco and follow the broad and level path onwards. The slopes are covered in ancient tree heather, laurel, bilberry and broom, with wooden fencing alongside. There are brief glimpses down into the valley, then cross a bouldery patch. The levada path appears to narrow, but in fact it remains broad as far as a viewpoint area with stone seating. There is a slender

The Levada das Vinte
Cinco Fontes, or Levada
of 25 Fountains

waterfall and a weeping wall in a sheer rock-walled
amphitheatre. Further access is prohibited, and the rocks
are dangerously slippery. Retrace steps to the junction.

Turn right downhill as signposted for 25 Fontes. There
are winding steps on the steep and wooded slope, then
land beside a levada and turn right. This is the Levada
das Vinte Cinco Fontes and the path is concrete. Cross a
bouldery gully and pass some pipework, then the path
narrows. Walk down steps and cross a wide bridge over
the bouldery Ribeira Grande, then climb up steps to join
the levada again. The path loops round the valley side
and sometimes leads along a buttressing wall, so use the
narrow levada parapet as a handrail. The stony surfaces
are uneven in places so take care. There are some views,
but mostly the tree heather is quite dense. Turn round a
tight bend on a spur and enter a side valley. Leave the
levada and divert up a bouldery streambed for a few
paces to see a streaming rock-walled amphitheatre at **25
Fontes**. There is a pool full of big boulders, springs feed it
with water – though maybe not as many as 25!

Transport:
Nova minibuses visit
Rabaçal, otherwise use a
taxi.

Refreshments:
None. The nearest place
is the Jungle Rain Café
on the ER-110 in the
direction of Paúl da
Serra.

Double back along the levada to reach the tight bend on the spur, then drop downhill and follow a zig-zag path through tall heather. Land beside the **Levada da Água do Vimieiro** where there is a cave. Turn right and follow the levada upstream. The path is good, but there is also a dripping cliff covered in liverworts where it could be slippery. Cut into a side valley, which is actually below 25 Fontes, and cross a levada stepping stone footbridge over a rocky gorge. There is also a tunnel at this point, but do not enter it. Continue along the narrow levada path, leaving the side valley, passing a small shrine where people leave a coin and offer a prayer. The path is mostly good, but exposed in places, though it sometimes has a vegetated edge. Turn round a couple of attractive rocky corners where there is a rocky lip. It is less exposed for a while, with a delightful edge of green turf and fine views along the Janela valley. After passing a spur dotted with odd pines and turning round a rocky corner, enter a denser stand of 'laurisilva'. Breaks in the vegetation reveal a side valley at **Adeneiro**. Walk as far as an exposed, narrow, concrete path with a waterfall ahead, then it is time to turn round and retrace steps.

Walk back along the levada to reach the cave where the levada was first joined, then continue walking downstream. Turn round a rocky corner into a rocky valley where there is a mixture of trees. Cut across the valley using a footbridge over rock pools in the Ribeira Grande. Follow a very stony path up a slope of bracken to leave the river, then zig-zag up a steep pitched path on a slope of tree heather and laurel. On reaching the Levada das Vinte Cinco Fontes, turn right to follow it downstream. The levada path is good and turns round corners to lead into the valley drained by the Ribeira do Alecrim. At this point the water flows through a pipeline and enters a huge **tunnel**; easily the biggest levada tunnel on Madeira. There is a cobbled path entering the tunnel and far more headroom than anyone needs. To walk through it, note that it is 800m (875yds) long and you have to come back the same way. To end the walk, climb up a nearby flight of stone steps to return to the houses and car park at **Rabaçal**.

Walk 31: Ponta do Pargo to Fonte do Bispo

THE ROUTE

Distance:
10km (6 miles).

Start:
At the lighthouse at Ponta do Pargo – 885326.

Finish:
On the ER-110 road near Fonte do Bispo – 959305.

Maps:
Military Survey 1:25,000 Sheet 1 or
IGC 1:50,000 Madeira West.

Terrain:
The ascent is along narrow roads and clear tracks.
Wooded slopes give way to open scrub moorland. The
walk ends on a road on a high crest.

This walk is relatively simple; from the Ponta do Pargo lighthouse at the extreme western end of Madeira, up to a high crest that leads to Paúl da Serra. Gradients are not too steep and the tracks used are not too stony, so taken steadily the ascent poses no problems even on a hot day. In mist, be careful at junctions of tracks, as the slopes are covered with a network that could be confusing. It is handy to be collected at the junction of the ER-110 and ER-210 roads near Fonte do Bispo, though it is also possible to walk back downhill afterwards.

The red and white lighthouse, or **Farol**, at Ponta do Pargo stands on 300m (1000ft) high cliffs at the extreme western end of Madeira. Follow the cliff-top road signposted for the Miradouro and Casa de Chá O Fío tea house. The road rises gently past experimental vineyards to reach the **tea house** and viewpoint. Enjoy the coastal views then follow the road a bit further uphill and inland. A concrete road continues past the buildings at Salão de Baixo to reach the church at **Ponta do Pargo.** There are toilets under the square in front of the church, and the Restaurante Solar do Pero is just across the road. Follow the road uphill from the church, passing the Bar Girassol. This road is the Rua Dr Vasco Augusta de Franca. Cross over the main ER-101 road, with the post office to the right and Bar Garrido to the left.

Follow a concrete road uphill, swinging right and later left to climb past the last houses and leave the village. Pass a tall wall and rock cutting, then join a

Transport:
Rodoeste Bus 80 and
107 serves Ponta do
Pargo. Taxi from Fonte do
Bispo, or walk back
downhill.

Refreshments:
There are a few bars and
restaurants around Ponta
do Pargo.

*On the track that leads
upwards towards Fonte
do Bispo*

tarmac road and continue up a slope of tall pines to a **water works**. The road swings right, and steps on the left reach the Levada Calheta – Ponta do Pargo. Turn right to walk upstream, crossing little cattle grids to enter and leave a field. Turn left up a concrete road, and continue up a clear, sunken dirt track into pine and eucalyptus. Note the scorched trunks, pointing to a fire in the past. Bracken and gorse form the undergrowth. Another track rises from the left, but keep climbing, avoiding lesser tracks, sometimes in deep clay cuttings. One of these cuttings has hollowed-out caves to the left. There is a small levada to the left and a cattle grid is crossed at a fork. Keep right, climbing among tall pines with plenty of clearance between them. Other tracks converge on the main track, then cross a hump and descend a little. Keep left to start climbing again, always following the broadest and clearest track uphill. The pine cover is sparse and the trees eventually peter out on extensive slopes of bracken. The summit to the left is the **Alto da Ponta do Pargo**, rising to 998m (3274ft).

Cattle and goats may be noticed after climbing a little further, grazing areas of grass among the bracken. The track levels out and swings round to the right, onto the other side of the valley, even descending slightly. Tall heather, bilberry and gorse flank the track in places. Watch for a track off to the left, climbing uphill, then swinging to the right, then left again. It appears to join another clear track, but this is the same as the one that was being following earlier, with a loop cut from it. The track rises further, crossing broken rock at one point, and bracken gives way to clumps of heather. The track undulates gently, with tall heather alongside, then one final pull, keeping left at a fork, leads up to the ER-110 road. Turning right, there is a junction with signposts at 1230m (4035ft) indicating **Fonte do Bispo**, Prazéres, Paúl da Serra, Canhas and Porto Moniz. Arrange to be collected here to finish the walk quickly. It is not a long or difficult ascent, and it is also possible to walk back down to Ponta do Pargo. Close by, but for another day, is the start of Walk 32 down to Porto Moniz.

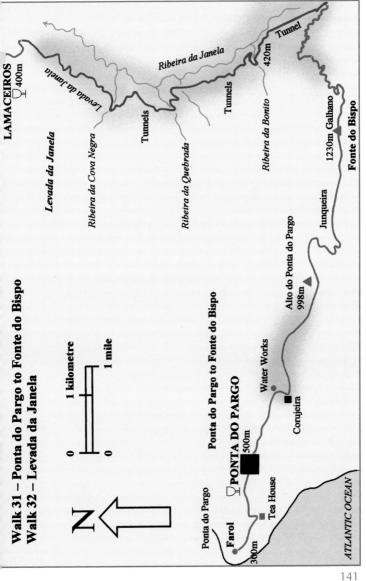

Walk 31 – Ponta do Pargo to Fonte do Bispo
Walk 32 – Levada da Janela

Ponta do Pargo to Fonte do Bispo

LAMACEIROS 400m

Ribeira da Janela

Tunnel

420m

Levada da Janela

Ribeira da Cova Negra

Tunnels

Ribeira da Quebrada

Tunnels

Ribeira da Bonito

1230m Galhano

Fonte do Bispo

Junqueira

Alto do Ponta do Pargo 998m

Water Works

PONTA DO PARGO 500m

Corujeira

Ponta do Pargo

Farol

300m

Tea House

ATLANTIC OCEAN

N

0   1 kilometre
0   1 mile

141

WALK 32: Levada da Janela

One of the most interesting and exciting levadas is absent from most maps. The Levada da Janela draws water from a deep and wooded valley in the north-west of the island, and feeds the Central da Ribeira da Janela generating station. Although the levada can be reached easily from Lamaceiros above Porto Moniz, following it into the valley means retracing steps later. Start high at Fonte do Bispo, however, to walk down a steep track and path almost to the source of the levada, then follow it downstream to Lamaceiros. Note that the walk includes eight tunnels, and one of them is long and wet!

THE ROUTE

Distance:
16km (10 miles).

Start:
On the ER-110 road near Fonte do Bispo – 959305.

Finish:
Lamaceiros above Porto Moniz – 973369.

Maps:
Military Survey 1:25,000 Sheet 1 or IGC 1:50,000 Madeira West.

Terrain:
The descent is on a stony or grassy track and a steep and crumbling path. The levada goes through eight tunnels, including a very long and wet one. Some parts of the path are exposed, but the slopes are mostly wooded.

Start high on the ER-110 road near **Fonte do Bispo**, where there is a signpost at 1230m (4035ft) pointing along a track for **Galhano**. The track is grassy and rises slightly, then descends through chained gateposts and is stonier, with rough concrete strips. Cross a cattle grid and pass plenty of tree heather, laurel and tall bilberry, with some broom and candleberry. There is good shade and occasional views across to Fanal on the far side of the valley. Pass a huddle of beehives and walk down into denser, taller tils, where it is quite dark at times. Emerge at a small rock cutting and a little wooden hut.

A narrow path runs behind the hut, steep and stony, with an open stretch subject to landslips. Cross a small concrete footbridge over a rocky gorge, then pick a way across the base of a cliff, rising gently. Walk downhill again on a series of battered wooden steps. There is dense til woodland on a steep slope. Take care, though there are a few more substantial concrete and stone steps later, then a final series of battered steps lead down to the Levada da Janela. Cross over and turn left to walk downstream. The altitude is around 420m (1380ft).

Reach a **tunnel** mouth and reach for a torch. There is good headroom and a good path, though it slopes towards the water. Exit into a deep, rocky, wooded gorge, then enter the next **tunnel**. This is a long one; measuring 1.2km (¾ mile). There is good headroom for the most part, though the path is narrow at the start. Later, the path is wider, but uneven and bouldery in places. There are constant showers from cracks in the roof, and a vicious 'power shower' from a crack in the rock wall to the right. Expect to be very wet when leaving the tunnel, using a much better path. Emerge in a wooded side valley and the levada goes through a rock arch and continues with an overhanging lip where it is been cut from a rock-face. Note the lovely ferns alongside on leaving the valley, and swing round into another side valley. Cross a rustic footbridge over the **Ribeira do Bonito** and notice the coverings over the levada to catch landslip debris. There is a tremendous view through the main Janela valley, taking in the riverbed, steep wooded slopes and thick beds of volcanic boulders.

Go through a short **tunnel**. There are a couple of squeezes, but otherwise no problems. Curve round a rock wall and enter another **tunnel**, using a torch again. There is low headroom in places and a narrow path. Exit and continue along a broad path, which narrows and leads into another little side valley. Cross a small wooden footbridge. A narrow levada path leads out of the valley and it is partly fenced as it crosses a wooded, rocky slope high above the Ribeira da Janela. There are splendid valley views and an easy stretch of path, then another short **tunnel**. This one has a low entry and exit, but good headroom in between. The path in the tunnel is good, but narrow. Walk a short way across a slope to reach the next **tunnel**, which is longer, so use a torch again. It has good headroom most of the time, but beware of projecting rock. The path can be narrow, but is mostly good. Emerge in a tight little side valley with plenty of

Transport:
Taxi to Fonte do Bispo.
Rodoeste Bus 80 serves
Lamaceiros.

Refreshments:
There is a small bar at
the end at Lamaceiros.

The densely wooded and steep-sided valley of Ribeira da Janela

ferns, and leave by following a narrow, fenced path. The woodlands are 'laurisilva' but the levada has a border of hydrangeas. Swing round into the main Janela valley again and pass a levada keeper's cottage.

Walk round into another side valley, passing a dripping cliff covered in ferns, mosses and liverworts. Leave this valley and turn round into the next little valley, where there are awesome rock walls on both sides, and no room for a path beside the levada. Instead, the levada is covered with concrete slabs, so walk on them. Enter the penultimate **tunnel**. There is good headroom and a good path, but there are puddles in the middle. Swing to the right to exit, and be ready for low headroom and lots of drips. It might be dripping on the path outside the tunnel, and there may even be a waterfall. Use the levada stepping stones and go through a shelter to avoid the worst of the water. The path is fenced round a sheer-sided valley head, then go through the final **tunnel**. It is a bit wet and muddy, but mostly has a good path, though it is narrow and has low headroom in places. The levada swings left at the end, and enters a rather tight, fern-covered, wooded side valley. Follow the levada path onwards.

The path is mostly fenced leaving the side valley, then swings round overlooking the main Janela valley. Enter a much more densely wooded side valley, and leaving this, walk round into a wet and dripping side valley, crossing the bouldery head before leaving. There is a rock cutting to walk through while returning to the main valley, where a couple of small concrete huts are passed. The levada has no fencing, but is not particularly exposed either. There are glimpses down the valley to houses at Ribeira da Janela from a picnic table. The levada widens to a deep trough, and there is a sudden mixture of trees and shrubs, including hydrangeas and apples alongside. Pass a concrete overspill and walk back into dense laurel, then pass another viewpoint with a picnic bench. There is tall eucalyptus alongside the levada, and the grassy path is fringed with hydrangeas and agapanthus. Tall pines and eucalyptus grow above the levada, then there is a water intake and street lights lead to a road. Turn left up the road to reach a junction, then turn right to walk down to the village of **Lamaceiros**. Buses are limited at this point, though taxis in Porto Moniz are only a phone call away. Take a break in a small bar while waiting.

WALK 33: Levada Calheta – Ponta do Pargo – part 1

Here is a levada that can be followed a long way, and it is largely free of other walkers. The Levada Calheta – Ponta do Pargo, including every loop of its convoluted course, is around 60km (37 miles). Some maps call it the Levada Nova, though other levadas also have that name. It runs at an altitude of around 630–650m (2065–2130ft). It can be split into three sections, omitting the extreme ends of the channel, and this first stretch is from Ponta do Pargo to Prazéres. There are plenty of settlements along the way, with wooded valleys between. If you are staying in Prazéres, there is need to hurry for a bus at the end.

THE ROUTE

Distance:
20km (12¾ miles).

Start:
Ponta do Pargo – 902322.

Finish:
Prazéres – 941260.

Maps:
Military Survey 1:25,000 Sheets 1 and 4 or IGC 1:50,000 Madeira West.

Terrain:
The initial ascent is by road, then the path is level and easy, crossing cultivated slopes, passing villages and turning well-wooded valley heads.

Start at a crossroads in **Ponta do Pargo**, where the post office and Bar Garrido are located. Follow a concrete road from the crossroads, swinging right and later left to climb past the last houses and leave the village. Pass a tall wall and rock cutting, then join a tarmac road and continue up a slope of tall pines to a water works. The road swings right, and steps on the left reach the Levada Calheta – Ponta do Pargo. Turn right to walk upstream, crossing little cattle grids to enter and leave a field. Cross a concrete road and continue through an earth cutting. Cross a cultivated slope and go through a tiny rock cutting, reaching a wooded slope of oaks, pines and apples while turning round a little valley. Walk round the head of another little valley and cross a slope of pines that have charred trunks. Bracken and brambles grow beside the levada, as well as a few hydrangeas. Cross a bit of a track when swinging out of the valley, then cross a road above the village of **Amparo.**

Walk past plots of fruit and vegetables and cross another slope of pines, as well as oaks, chestnuts and apples. Turn round the head of a valley drained by the Ribeira dos Câmbios and cross a grassy track. Turn round into the next valley, which has a few charred pines and bracken on one side, while the other side is covered in eucalyptus. Pass a few chestnuts while leaving the valley. The levada is covered as it passes buildings at Lombo and crosses a narrow road, then there is a short, narrow rock cutting. Take care walking on uneven slabs and pass a couple more houses. Cross a short levada bridge and pass chestnuts and apples before crossing the ER-101 road. The Café Bar Achada is just up the road if required. There are tall pines, eucalyptus and bracken on the slope. A grassy track crosses the levada and the path is flanked by agapanthus and apples. Cross another grassy track and there is a view back to the lighthouse, or Farol, near Ponta do Pargo. The next slope has tangled undergrowth and there are a few pines and chestnuts dotted across it. Turn right round a valley below a bend on the ER-101 road. There are mixed woods for a short way, then cross a track and swing round a cultivated spur. Go up a track and down a few steps, then round a corner along a concrete path. Follow an earth path across a cultivated slope, then the levada is partly covered until it reaches a narrow concrete road. Either walk up to the Bar os Marinheiros at **Lombada dos Marinheiros**, or simply walk straight across the ER-101 road below the village.

There is a viewpoint picnic site beside the road, looking down the deep-cut Marinheiros valley to the sea. The levada cuts across a slope and proceeds into the higher, wonderfully wooded parts of the valley to cross a levada stepping stone footbridge. Leave the valley and cross the ER-101 road, then the levada is stoutly buttressed. Make a series of little loops across the slope, passing a few tall pines and odd chestnuts before crossing a narrow concrete track above a house where vines grow. Bracken and brambles grow alongside the levada, then cross a steep and narrow road at Casa da Levada, between **São João** and Fajã da Ovelha. Turn a corner for a view of settlements stretching all the way to Raposeira, but it takes time to get there.

Transport:
Rodoeste Bus 80 and 107 serve Ponta do Pargo and Prazéres.

Refreshments:
Bars offer food and drink at Ponta do Pargo, Lombada dos Marinheiros, Raposeira and Prazéres.

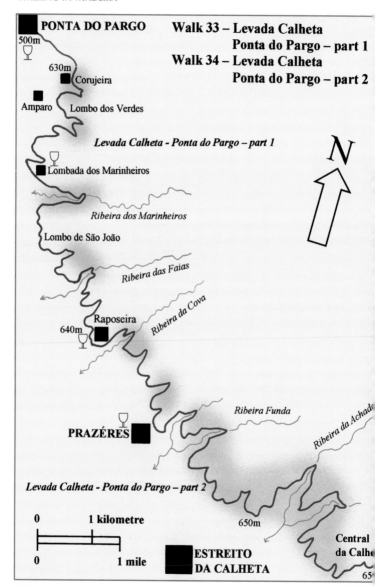

PONTA DO PARGO

500m

630m
Corujeira

Amparo

Lombo dos Verdes

Walk 33 – Levada Calheta
Ponta do Pargo – part 1
Walk 34 – Levada Calheta
Ponta do Pargo – part 2

Levada Calheta - Ponta do Pargo – part 1

N

Lombada dos Marinheiros

Ribeira dos Marinheiros

Lombo de São João

Ribeira das Faias

Ribeira da Cova

Raposeira

640m

Ribeira Funda

Ribeira da Achado

PRAZÉRES

Levada Calheta - Ponta do Pargo – part 2

0   1 kilometre

0   1 mile

650m

ESTREITO
DA CALHETA

Central
da Calhe

65

Cross a cultivated slope, then climb steps up to a concrete road. Walk down a bit, then walk up a narrow ramp to the right of a gateway to regain the levada. Cultivated slopes give way to pines round a double valley head, where the Ribeira de São João is crossed. Walk across a slope of bracken and pines to leave the valley, and admire the flowery borders at the houses at São Lourenço. Cross a tarmac road, go through a little cutting, cross a concrete road and pass a water regulator. Follow a wider, deeper stretch of the levada. Walk round into the next valley, across a slope of charred pines, and cross the road that serves Paúl do Mar. Walk up the road a bit before stepping down onto the levada. There is a shop/bar up the road in Lombada dos Cedros.

It is tangled and wooded while walking round double valley heads and crossing two levada stepping stone footbridges over the **Ribeira das Faias**. The main road is just above while passing small vegetable plots and a few trees. Cross a concrete track and swing round into the next valley. This is only a small valley with a few trees, then swing past a house and reach a cobbled road. Turn left uphill, then right down steps to regain the levada. Pass a few tall pines and some old, overgrown terraces. Turn round the head of another valley and pass a few more tall pines. Leave the valley and swing round the slope, follow a broad concrete path, passing fruit and vegetables, then cross a concrete road. Follow a concrete path to a road, where the levada is signposted off to the left. It is tightly enclosed on the way to the next tarmac road. If a break is needed, then walk up the road, to find the Bar Gomes at the top, not far from the church in the little village of **Raposeira**.

The levada is covered where it leaves the road, then it flows through more cultivated country as it describes an arc across the slope below the church. Agapanthus grows alongside the path and there are mixed woods either side of the ER-101 road. There is a wonderful mixture of trees and shrubs round a little valley, then on the way to the next little valley, tall pines dominate. Cross the **Ribeira da Cova** using a levada stepping stone footbridge and follow the path onwards. Cross a minor road

The twin spired church at Prazéres where you can take a break in the village

just above the main road and continue past houses. Cross another road and walk past more buildings. Turn into the next valley at Poço Grande, where there are tall pines around the top. Cross another two levada stepping stone footbridges, then pass a few chestnuts on the way out of the valley. Agapanthus lines the path the whole way round. Cross a tarmac road close to the main road at Lombo do Coelho.

Leaving Lombo there are apple trees near the path. Make a tight turn around a little valley full of chestnuts, laurels and brambles, then There is a junction near the main road with a picnic site below. Continue along the levada into another valley full of tall pines and chestnuts, and cross the Ribeira Seca. The levada runs into a road at Lombo da Velha. Walk straight through a crossroads to continue along the ER-101 road. The levada heads away to the left, passing vegetable plots and turning round a little valley full of tall pines. Leaving the valley, follow the path past a water regulator, where the levada is again broader and deeper. Beyond is a road and picnic benches beside the Posto Florestal **Prazéres**. Turn right down the road to reach a crossroads on the ER-101 road. Wander round the village to find a selection of bars and restaurants.

WALK 34: Levada Calheta – Ponta do Pargo – part 2

THE ROUTE

Distance:
19km (12 miles).

Start:
Prazéres – 941260.

Finish:
On the ER-222 road at Ribeira da Atouguia – 987233.

Maps:
Military Survey 1:25,000 Sheet 4 or
IGC 1:50,000 Madeira West.

Terrain:
The levada path is level and easy, looping round open slopes and wooded valleys away from habitations. There is a descent by road at the end.

Start at a crossroads on the main ER-101 road in **Prazéres**. There are small shops and bars offering food or drink before starting. Follow the road signposted uphill for Paúl da Serra to reach the Posto Florestal **Prazéres** beside the Levada Calheta – Ponta do Pargo. Turn left to follow the flow upstream. Agapanthus and hydrangeas line the path across a slope of charred pines. There is also oak, laurel and eucalyptus, with a brambly ground cover. Turning round the head of the valley is like walking in a jungle. Walk out of the valley and round into the next valley, which is mostly filled with tall pines and eucalyptus, interspersed with chestnuts later, with tall heather on rocky parts. Cross the bouldery bed of the **Ribeira Funda** at the head of the valley. There are tall trees on the way out of the valley, turning a couple of corners and crossing a track on the Lombo da Ribeira Funda.

Follow the levada in loops across a wooded slope, then pass a water works where the levada is briefly

The middle part of the Levada Calheta – Ponta do Pargo is surprisingly removed from habitations. Leaving Prazéres the levada loops further and further away from the road, so there are only glimpses of the well-populated and cultivated slopes around Calheta. Instead there are well-wooded valleys and a few open slopes too. Trees may be indigenous in remote enclaves, but often the woods are eucalyptus and pines. The levada is quite large at the end of the walk, and carries a considerable flow. The Central da Calheta generating station uses water from the mountains, which is then channelled west and east for irrigation.

Transport:
Rodoeste Bus 80 and
107 serve Prazéres and
Calheta. Taxis at Calheta.

Refreshments:
There are a couple of
bars and restaurants at
Prazéres, as well as off-
route along the road at
Calheta at the end.

covered at the keeper's house. The channel is wider and deeper further upstream. Pass pines and eucalyptus and cross a track, followed by a small concrete bridge. Pass some fenced fruit plots, then there are tall, charred pines and eucalyptus. The levada continues describing loops, then there is a short and narrow cutting, and another track to cross. There are a couple of tin-roofed buildings below, and old terracing. The grass beneath the trees is used for grazing. Cross another track on the Lombo das Castanheiros and swing round into a big valley. There are views across the valley to slopes full of houses at Calheta.

Go through a rickety gate to enter the valley, turning round a corner to pass a small tin hut. The path narrows, so watch your step. Look out for laurel among the eucalyptus and pines. Pass another tin hut and cross the head of the valley, where the **Ribeira da Achada** has a rocky bed and is hemmed in by hills. There is a mixture of laurel, tree heather and candleberry, but this quickly gives way to eucalyptus and tall, charred pines again. The path narrows on a steep and rocky slope, but it is not too exposed. There is a pronounced turn round the Lombo Grande into the next valley. Pass another tin hut among tall, burnt trees. There are some chestnuts, and a little side valley features tufts of heather. Continue past a fine variety of trees and shrubs, turning round the head of the valley and crossing the Ribeira do Raposo. There is yet another tin hut beside the levada on the way out of the valley. Eucalyptus is dominant at first, followed by tall pines. The levada swings out of the valley and goes through a little cutting, staying among tall trees. Walk round a couple of smaller valleys, crossing a track between them, then pass a concrete reservoir. Follow a concrete path, then the levada channel is covered in big slabs. A very steep and patchy road offers a rapid descent to Calheta if needed.

Cross over the road to continue and the levada flows through a big concrete trough. Sometimes it is covered with slabs and sometimes it is open as it turns round a small, wooded valley full of eucalyptus and pine. There are steps up and down while crossing an old, cobbled road. Keep following the concrete trough across the slope, sometimes on a concrete path, or with wooden fencing alongside. The slope is steep and grassy with a few trees. There is a tight little turn round a side valley, then the levada runs into tall pines, with a few eucalyptus and mimosa. At the **Central da Calheta** generating station, climb up a flight of steps, cross a dam on the Ribeira da Calheta and walk behind the building. To finish the walk, simply follow the cobbled road downhill to reach the main ER-222 road below, which has a bus service. Arrange to be collected at the Central da Calheta generating station and you save the final 2.5km (1½ mile) walk down the road.

WALK 35: Levada Calheta – Ponta do Pargo – part 3

THE ROUTE
Distance:
23km (14¼ miles).
Start:
On the ER-222 road at Ribeira da Atouguia – 987233.
Finish:
In the middle of Ponta do Sol – 030174.
Maps:
Military Survey 1:25,000 Sheets 4, 5 and 8 or IGC 1:50,000 Madeira West.
Terrain:
The levada path is mostly level and easy, with wooded valleys and cultivated slopes. The path in the Madalena valley is exposed in places. There is a descent along steep roads at the end.

Start on the ER-222 road where it crosses the Ribeira da Atouguia near Calheta. A road uphill is signposted for the **Central da Calheta** generating station. Hiring a taxi from Calheta to the station saves a 2.5km (1½ miles) walk up the road. Approach the generating station along the

The eastern stretch of the Levada Calheta – Ponta do Pargo runs from the Central da Calheta generating station to a point high above the steep-sided Ponta do Sol valley. The route passes a few farming communities, but is well above the villages along the main road. There are a number of little valleys along the way, and the levada loops in and out of them. It also works its way round the magnificent Madalena valley, which is unknown to most walkers. When the levada finally reaches the Ponta do Sol valley, descend along a series of steep roads to end at Ponta do Sol.

153

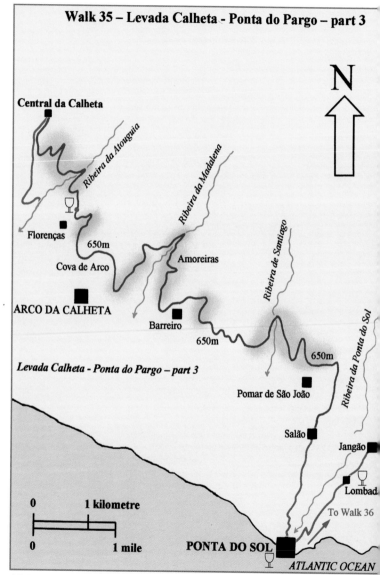

Walk 35 – Levada Calheta - Ponta do Pargo – part 3

N

Central da Calheta

Ribeira da Atouguia

Florenças

650m

Cova de Arco

Ribeira da Madalena

Amoreiras

ARCO DA CALHETA

Barreiro

Ribeira de Santiago

650m

650m

Levada Calheta - Ponta do Pargo – part 3

Pomar de São João

Ribeira da Ponta do Sol

Salão

Jangão

Lombad

0   1 kilometre

0   1 mile

To Walk 36

PONTA DO SOL

ATLANTIC OCEAN

cobbled road and the Levada Calheta – Ponta do Pargo slices off sharply to the right. The channel is wide and deep and it is followed downstream. First, walk along a wall between the levada and the road, then follow an earth path into mixed woods with agapanthus alongside. Cross an old cobbled road that is rather overgrown and swing round into a little valley. There are charred pines and a few cultivation terraces, as well as buildings while crossing another cobbled road on the Lombo da Atouguia.

Head into the next little valley, which is well wooded with a mixture of trees. Cross a levada stepping stone footbridge over the Ribeira do Luis and walk out of the valley. Note the little storage sheds dotted all over the terraces. Cross a levada stepping stone footbridge over a wooded gully on the way round into the next valley. There is a mixture of trees in the valley. Cross a concrete slab footbridge over the Ribeira das Faias at its head. Pass pines and chestnuts on the way out of the valley, then walk through a shallow cutting lined with agapanthus. Cross a concrete track and swing round into the next little valley at Faias, which is well cultivated. Cross a tarmac road and continue along the path, where views reveal well-settled slopes around Calheta. Cross a concrete road above **Florenças**. There is a small bar just uphill, or simply continue straight through a short and easy tunnel through the ridge and walk into the next valley.

Cultivated slopes give way to a levada stepping stone footbridge at the head of the valley, crossing the Ribeira das Meninas. There are tall pines on leaving the valley, then pass circular water tanks and the keeper's cottage, where hydrangeas grow alongside the path. Cross a road at Achada da Cima and continue through tall pines, with agapanthus beside the path and hydrangeas across the levada. The trees thin out to give a grand view over the well settled hollow of **Arco da Calheta**. Pass a water regulator, followed by a steep, cobbled road, then continue along the levada where it is covered in slabs and passes through a small cutting. Soon afterwards, the channel crosses a cliff face and the parapet is narrow. Uneven slabs cover the levada, so take care as some are

Transport:
Rodoeste Bus 80 and 107 serve Calheta. Taxis at Calheta. Rodoeste Bus 4, 80 and 107 serve Ponta do Sol. Taxis at Ponta do Sol.

Refreshments:
There are only a couple of bars along the way, but there are several bars and restaurants in Ponta do Sol.

A 'levada stepping stone footbridge' takes the levada over a river

broken or missing. An easier path continues past tall eucalyptus and pines with charred trunks. Turn through a little cutting where the levada goes under a rough track and is covered with slabs, then there is a glimpse down to Madalena do Mar before entering the large Madalena valley.

Cross a slope of eucalyptus and mimosa, then there is a narrow parapet path and the scale of the valley becomes apparent. Rock overhangs the levada in places, and there is a small, curved **tunnel**, with a good path and good headroom. Immediately afterwards, the channel is covered with slabs, and other stretches are covered when the levada has cliffs above and below. Watch your feet and beware of gaps, holes and rockfalls. Turn round a rugged side valley, with rock walls and mixed woods, featuring laurel and heather. Drop down a path with steps and cross a concrete slab footbridge, then climb up steps to avoid a narrow and slippery parapet at the head of the valley. Walk back into the main valley, crossing slopes of fruit and vegetables and passing farm buildings, where the channel is again covered for short stretches. The head of the **Madalena** valley is wilder, with an undercut dripping cliff and narrow parapet in places, but it is not particularly exposed. There are plenty of laurels, then cross a levada stepping stone footbridge over a bouldery gorge. There are lovely ferns in this dark and damp recess.

Walk away from the head of the valley, passing well-wooded cliffs, featuring pine and eucalyptus. The path is exposed for short stretches, but some parts are fenced. Turn into a side valley full of eucalyptus and pines, and cross a levada stepping stone footbridge over a deep, narrow, fern-covered gorge. Leave the side valley and return to the main Madalena valley, where the levada is covered in slabs and earth. It is exposed for a bit, then less exposed as heather, agapanthus, broom and odd pines rise alongside. The scale of the valley can be appreciated now you have walked round it. Turn left to walk among tall pines and the levada is uncovered again on the way downstream. There are gentle and partly cultivated slopes around **Barreiro** e Feiteiras. Cross a road, then a house sits on the levada, so keep to the perimeter of the garden wall, on the downhill side, to rejoin the flow.

Walk round a large cultivated hollow and cross another road, passing houses and following a concrete path. A narrow earth path leads to a tight turn round the uncultivated head of the valley. Cross a levada stepping stone footbridge over the Ribeira do Carvalhal. The slope is largely covered in pines on leaving the valley, but there is a mixture of trees. Pass above a church and school at Carvalhal, then in the next cultivated hollow, the levada goes under a vegetable plot, under a concrete road and under slabs to pass a house. The path runs downhill to avoid a narrow parapet, so climb up steps later to continue. There is a levada stepping stone footbridge over a concrete road, then other parts of the channel are under concrete. Cross a tarmac road to continue past a circular water tank. A concrete path leads past houses, and even when it becomes an earth path there are street lights alongside.

The levada swings into a little valley full of pines and eucalyptus, then on leaving the valley there is a view for a while. Cross a road and another levada stepping stone footbridge. Pass vegetable plots and cross another steep road, then walk into the Santiago valley. This is clothed in eucalyptus, pine and mimosa. At its head, make a tight turn across the **Ribeira de Santiago**. The woodlands are quite dense and mixed on leaving the valley, but many parts are dominated by eucalyptus. Cross a dirt track, then cross a cobbled track on the Lombo de São João, still in tall eucalyptus. The next valley has a mixture of chestnut and eucalyptus. Turn round its head to cross the Ribeiro de São João. On the way out of the valley, pass pines, eucalyptus, chestnut and mimosa. The houses at **Pomar de São João** are seen below. Cross a steep concrete road and pass a water regulator and a square concrete tank. A track continues beside the levada, with agapanthus alongside, then head downhill and turn right down a concrete and cobbled track.

The track runs along a crest covered in pines. Pass a water tank and descend with a levada chattering alongside. Follow a road downhill, then switch to a steeper concrete road on the right. This leads down to a junction where the walk continues straight down the steepest concrete road, with steps built into it. Go straight down through a crossroads at **Salão** and pass a church. Continue straight down the steepest tarmac road, on a slope covered in bananas. At sharp bends it is usually possible to cut straight through using concrete tracks and paths. This is especially the case when the road makes really wide bends towards the end. Landing on the ER-222 road, bear in mind that it has a bus service, otherwise, continue down steep roads and flights of steps all the way to **Ponta do Sol**. There are plenty of bars and restaurants if food and drink are needed before catching a bus, and there are taxis if you arrive late in the day.

WALK 36: Levada Nova – Ponta do Sol

THE ROUTE

Distance:
23km (14¼ miles), but note the alternatives.

Start:
In the middle of Ponta do Sol – 030174.

Finish:
By the sea at Ribeira Brava – 067162.

Maps:
Military Survey 1:25,000 Sheets 5 and 8 or IGC
1:50,000 Madeira West.

Terrain:
Steep concrete roads and steps are used for the ascent
and descent at the beginning and end. The levada has a
very exposed optional spur, but otherwise has a level,
easy path and crosses cultivated and wooded slopes.

The Levada Nova loops through lovely cultivated valleys high above Ponta do Sol and Ribeira Brava. It runs at an average altitude of 400m (1310ft), and some walkers may wish to get a taxi up to Jangão, though it is quite interesting to climb up the old roads to Jangão from Ponta do Sol. Make another decision at the village. Either start by following an exceedingly exposed stretch of the Levada Nova to its source, then return the same way, or simply omit that part and follow the easier part of the levada to a point high above Ribeira Brava. Steep roads and flights of steps lead downhill at the end.

Start in the middle of **Ponta do Sol,** which is hemmed in tightly between rocky headlands. Walk out of town as if heading for the main road and tunnel to Funchal, but swing sharply right to climb up a steep and rough road carved from a cliff. At the top, climb up steps and continue across the headland for a view of the cliff coast on the other side. Turn left inland, following a narrow concrete road up to a junction at bend on the ER-222 road. Cross the road with care and continue straight up a quieter road. There is a little church off to the right, but keep straight on passing houses all the way along the Lombada Ponta do Sol. The road levels out later and reaches a junction.

Keep straight on along the road, turning left to climb up another road, and left again to follow a steep concrete road with steps in the middle. Climb past houses and bananas to reach a pleasant square between a church

Walk 36 – Levada Nova
Walk 37 – Lombo do Mouro

Boca da Encume

10

Paúl da Serra

ER-110 Road

Tunnels

Pico das Furnas

1300m
Lombo do Mouro

Lombo do Mouro

Ribeira da Ponta do Sol

400m

Levada do Lombo do Mouro

Pico Queimado

Levada Nova

Levada Nova   Tábua

Levada Nova

810m

Jangão

Ribeira da Tábua

400m

Ribeira Brava

600m
Bar

From
Ponta do Sol

Bar   400m

Apresentação

Bar

N

0   1 kilometre

0   1 mil

ATLANTIC OCEAN

RIBEIRA BRAVA

and school at **Lombada**. The school building was once one of the biggest houses on the island, standing on an estate dating from the first settlement of Madeira. There is a small bar nearby if a break is needed. Walk past the church and turn left to continue climbing along a much narrower concrete path and steps, sometimes squeezing between the houses along the crest. Reach a road-end and keep walking straight onwards, and watch out for a flight of steps on the left, climbing up to the Levada Nova at Jangão. A taxi up to **Jangão** saves 3km (2 miles).

Turn left or right along the levada. Left leads upstream along an exceedingly exposed stretch of the levada to its source, where it draws water from the Ribeira Ponta do Sol. Heading that way means returning later to this point. Omit this spur and turn right to walk downstream instead saves 8km (5 miles).

Turning left to walk the optional spur, the levada is covered in uneven slabs until leaving the houses and entering the splendid deep-cut valley beyond. Note how exposed and crumbling the path is, but other parts are safer and more vegetated. Bear in mind that there are much more exposed stretches later. When the levada curves to the left under a rocky cutting, watch your head and take in the view down the valley to Ponta do Sol. After a drippy bit and a small waterfall where the path is slippery, there is a more exposed curve to the left under another rock cutting. This time, looking down the valley, views stretch only to the church at Lombada. There are more exposed stretches then there is more tree cover, including laurel and candleberry. Turn round a corner into a rocky hollow full of chestnuts. Turn round another corner into a rocky hollow where there is a tunnel. Bend to enter as it is quite low, but once inside there is good headroom and a good path, but a torch is needed. Exit into a rocky gorge with a waterfall pouring down to the right. Go through a rock arch and behind the waterfall, and cross three slabs laid over the levada where there is a constant shower of drips. Expect to get wet and be very careful of slippery surfaces. An exposed path leads out of the gorge, then it is less exposed and more vegetated back in the main valley. Pass a water regulator and

Transport:
Rodoeste Bus 4, 80 and 107 serve Ponta do Sol. Rodoeste Bus 4, 6, 7, 80, 107 and 139 serve Ribeira Brava. Taxis at Ponta do Sol and Ribeira Brava.

Refreshments:
There are bars and restaurants at Ponta do Sol and Ribeira Brava at the beginning and end of the walk. There are also small bars at Lombada and near the end of the levada above Ribeira Brava.

continue following the levada to its source by the **Ribeira da Ponta do Sol**. This is an area of lush grass, heather and broom, with trees including laurel, chestnut, eucalyptus and pine. When you are ready, turn around and retrace steps carefully to Jangão.

Walk through **Jangão**, crossing the steps that were first used to reach the Levada Nova, then follow a concrete path and cross a road. The levada leads past new houses. Go down a flight of steps to reach an older part of the village at a road junction. Go straight ahead along the road that runs gently up and out of the village, passing old and disused buildings. The levada is on the left of the road, then on the right, but do not try to reach it until there is a big flight of steps down to the right of the road near the head of the valley. Join the levada to turn round the head of the valley and cross a cultivated slope. Swing sharply into the next valley, crossing a narrow concrete path. The levada is covered in slabs where it passes a house, then it goes through a short tunnel with low headroom and a narrow path.

The path to the head of the valley is narrow and seems little used. It cuts across cultivation terraces and some are quite overgrown. Take care turning round the head of the valley, as the Ribeira da Caixa spills over the path as a waterfall and makes everything slippery. Pass slender willow and cross other overgrown and cultivated terraces. Walk along a short wall, then cross a slope of tall pines where agapanthus and brambles flank the levada. Leaving the valley, swing round and cross a tarmac road. Continue along a concrete path, then leave the levada briefly where it flows under a house. Head up to the left to join a concrete road, then walk down a little and turn left to follow the water downstream again.

The levada passes houses and enters the next valley, passing a few pines and mimosa. Walk along a short concrete wall at one point and notice a cave cut into the hillside. Cross a gully full of rampant vegetation, then notice that street lights have been erected along part of the levada, leading to a solitary house on the next spur. Pass below the house, where brambles and rampant vegetation engulf the old terraces. There is an open slope,

The levada enters a small tunnel on the way round the Madalena valley

followed by a bit of shady woodland side valley. Swing round a rocky corner back into the main valley and the little hill of Terça is just below the levada.

There are a few pines on the slope, then another little rocky corner and a few more tall pines. Turn another rocky corner to enter a side valley full of eucalyptus, then continue across a cut in a rocky slope where there are brambles and malfurada bushes. There is a view of Tábua sitting below the steep and wooded valley sides. Enter another little side valley, and cross a slippery riverbed at its head. Leave the valley and cross a few terraces, then there is a metal footbridge over the Ribeira de Mijas Velhas. A short walk leads to the slippery bed of the **Ribeira da Tábua**, and there is a lot of bamboo growing alongside. Cross a tarmac road just below the little church at **Tábua**.

Walk through more bamboo and continue downstream beside the levada. There are tall pines and enough tree cover so that the valley road is only occasionally seen below. There are some short, exposed stretches of the levada, but often there is vegetation alongside. Big slabs cover the flow in a corner where there is a rock cutting. Brambles and agapanthus flank the path but there is another exposed stretch before a tunnel. No torch is needed and the path is fairly wide, but it is also uneven and there is low headroom, so take care. Emerge and walk along a concrete wall, then cross a road.

The levada continues with a few exposed stretches and there is a little rocky edge covered in mimosa, brambles and prickly pears. Take a good look at the view then leave the Tábua valley by crossing a gentle ridge. There is a little thatched building seen on entering the next gentle valley, while walking past terraces and vegetable plots. At a set of large steps rising to the left, walk up to a road and turn right to walk down the road for a while. The levada flows away to the left, so get back onto the path to follow it. Pass more vegetable plots and a house, then pass above the **Bar** Bilhar a Volta. Either walk down steps to reach the bar, or walk down steps and then walk up the road to avoid an exposed walk along the top of a concrete wall. Either way, cross the road to continue.

The levada is narrow in its final stages, with an earth or concrete path, crossing a few more terraces. A sign at a concrete road announces the end of the levada, and there is a small shop/**bar** at this point, as well as a big concrete water tank. Turn right down the road, which appears to end suddenly with a view of the sea, but it actually breaks into steep steps that wind down past a few houses to a small parking space. Continue down a slightly less steep concrete road, drifting to a steep valley edge, where there is a safety rail alongside. Briefly walk on tarmac further down, where there is a little shop/**bar** before the final part of the descent.

Keep straight onwards and the concrete road zig-zags and has steps built into it. The road actually turns into a flight of steps before landing on a hairpin bend above **Ribeira Brava**. Walk down the road a short way, then down another zig-zag flight of steps. Cross the old road bridge at the bottom to reach the town. Either head for the church and the square in front of it, or explore narrow cobbled streets. To catch a bus or hire a taxi, then walk to the seafront. There is also a tourist information centre in a stout, stone tower, as well as plenty of places offering food and drink.

The view eastwards along the cliff coast high above Ponta do Sol

WALK 37: Lombo do Mouro

The Lombo do Mouro is a long ridge offering a good walk mostly downhill. The upper part is reached by following the ER-110 road up from the Boca da Encumeada, then there is a walk down to the sea at Ribeira Brava. For the most part the Levada do Lombo do Mouro is followed, which flows quite vigorously as it descends. There are rough and stony mountainsides on the upper part of the route, followed by squeezes through dense eucalyptus woods for a while. There are some good paths and tracks, but sometimes the way is almost closed by trees. Steep roads and steps finally lead down to Ribeira Brava.

THE ROUTE
Distance:
15km (9½ miles).
Start:
Boca da Encumeada – 112255.
Finish:
By the sea at Ribeira Brava – 067162.
Maps:
Military Survey 1:25,000 Sheets 5 and 8 or IGC 1:50,000 Madeira West.
Terrain:
After an initial road-walk the path is quite rough and stony as it crosses steep slopes. Later the path is quite narrow as it passes through dense woods. Steep roads and steps complete the descent.

Start at the Snack Bar Restaurante **Encumeada**, around 1000m (3280ft), and walk through the rocky gap at the very top of the road. Turn left to follow the **ER-110 road**, signposted for Paúl da Serra and Lombo do Mouro. Climb gradually uphill, passing the Montanha Boutique souvenir shop and a roadside quarry. The road climbs through three **tunnels** and in between them, peer over the steep slope and enjoy views down the steep-sided valley and the mountains around. The road climbs more gently round a big hollow in the mountainside. Watch out for a bend where a sign reads **'Lombo do Mouro'**. Arrange for a lift to this point to save the 4km (2½ miles) road-walk from Encumeada. The altitude is nearly 1300m (4265ft).

Just before the sign, a path with wooden fencing leads steeply downhill in crooked zig-zags, landing beside the narrow **Levada do Lombo do Mouro**. The slope is rough and rocky, covered in bracken, broom and heather. Turn right to follow the path downstream beside the levada.

There is a house sitting on a gap nearby. The levada is more or less level as it cuts across the head of a steep-sided valley, but beware of rockfalls. Pass through a little gate and the path becomes easier as it continues gently downhill, flanked by bracken and the charred branches of former heather cover. The path swings out of the valley head and cuts across a rugged slope. As it picks up speed on an incline, the levada fairly chatters as it rushes downhill. Pumice and other stones rain down on the path from the cliff above, so take care. Pass a cave cut from the rock, and enjoy fine views down the valley to Serra de Água, as well as to the high mountains beyond. Walk down to a gate, then turn a corner, and go through a small rock cutting to cross a ridge. Descend along a grassy path on a slope of bracken and pass a few charred chestnuts. The levada reaches a valley that is densely wooded with eucalyptus and the path begins to squeeze between the trees. There was once a fire in this valley, and eucalyptus colonised the slopes. Watch out for fallen tree trunks and take care where undergrowth obscures the path. Later, the trees step back a bit and bracken covers a gentle gap on the ridge. Take a peek over to the right to spot the little village and church at **Tábua**.

Continue downstream, squeezing through broom and taking care where your unseen feet land. Things get easier while passing through a crumbling cutting, though the tree cover is as dense as ever. Exit left onto a track and turn right to follow it down to a very gentle gap on the crest. The track rises, then the course of the levada is followed again. The path is narrow and there are some charred and fallen tree trunks along the way, but there is less undergrowth. Walk through a bit of a cutting and swing right around a corner. Pass a few older trees clinging to life, including plane, chestnut and pine. The levada leads back onto the broad crest, passing mimosa and a few tall pines among the eucalyptus. The water suddenly rushes down through a cutting and continues alongside the track again, where there is now a good mixture of trees. Follow the levada through another cutting, then follow the track down to a road bend beside a circular reservoir tank.

Transport:

Rodoeste Bus 6 and 139 serve the Boca da Encumeada. Rodoeste Bus 4, 6, 7, 80, 107 and 139 serve Ribeira Brava. Taxis at Ribeira Brava.

Refreshments:

The Snack Bar Restaurante Encumeada is at the start of the walk. There is a small bar while crossing the Levada Nova on the descent. There are plenty of bars and restaurants in Ribeira Brava at the end.

167

Towards the end of the walk there's a steep descent to Ribeira Brava

Turn left down the road, then turn right down a steep concrete road. Head straight along a tarmac road beside an edge overlooking the steep-sided valley above Ribeira Brava. It is a long way down, so there is still quite a descent to complete. The road is at an altitude of 600m (1970ft). When the road swings to the right, it could be followed in long and lazy loops down to Ribeira Brava, but it takes a long time. Instead, cut off to the left, straight down a steep and narrow concrete road. There are a few houses on the top part of the road, but the middle part is flanked by mimosa and pines. Cross a tarmac road and walk down another concrete road. Cross the **Levada Nova**, which is followed in Walk 36, and there is a small shop/**bar** and a big concrete water tank at this point. The concrete road appears to end suddenly with a view of the sea, but it actually breaks into steep steps that wind down past a few houses to a small parking space.

Continue down a slightly less steep concrete road, drifting back to the valley edge, where there is a safety rail alongside. Briefly walk on tarmac further down, where there is a little shop/**bar** before the final part of the descent.

Keep straight onwards and the concrete road zig-zags and has steps built into it. The road actually turns into a flight of steps before landing on a hairpin bend above **Ribeira Brava**. Walk down the road a short way, then down another zig-zag flight of steps. Cross the old road bridge at the bottom to reach the town. Either head for the church and the square in front of it, or explore narrow cobbled streets. To catch a bus or hire a taxi, then walk to the seafront. There is also a tourist information centre in a stout, stone tower, as well as plenty of places offering food and drink.

WALK 38: Levada do Curral

THE ROUTE
Distance:
15km (9½ miles).
Start:
At the church in Curral das Freiras – 161216.
Finish:
On the Caminho de São Martinho in Funchal – 188137.
Maps:
Military Survey 1:25,000 Sheets 5, 8 and 9 or IGC 1:50,000 Madeira East & West.
Terrain:
The levada is mostly on a steep and wooded slope, but crosses sheer, exposed cliffs at times. Beware of rockfalls. At Fajã there are steep and slippery rocks. The final stretch through the suburbs of Funchal is much easier.

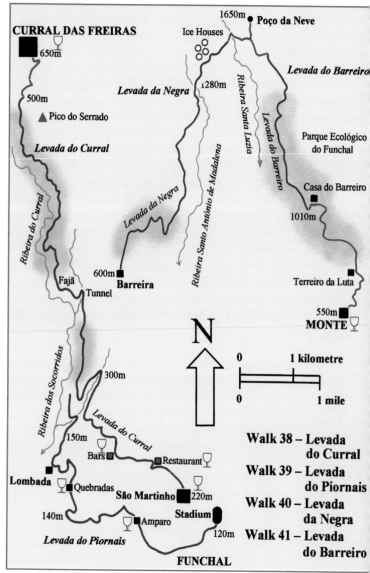

1650m **Poço da Neve**

Ice Houses

CURRAL DAS FREIRAS
650m

Levada do Barreiro

500m

1280m

▲ Pico do Serrado

Levada da Negra

Ribeira Santa Luzia

Levada do Barreiro

Levada do Curral

Parque Ecológico do Funchal

Ribeira do Curral

Levada da Negra

Ribeira Santo António de Madalena

Casa do Barreiro

1010m

Fajã

Tunnel

600m
Barreira

Terreiro da Luta

550m
MONTE

N

Ribeira dos Socorridos

300m

0   1 kilometre

0   1 mile

150m
Bars

Levada do Curral

Restaurant

Lombada

Quebradas

São Martinho 220m

Stadium

140m

Amparo

120m

Levada do Piornais

FUNCHAL

Walk 38 – Levada do Curral

Walk 39 – Levada do Piornais

Walk 40 – Levada da Negra

Walk 41 – Levada do Barreiro

Start at the church in **Curral das Freiras** and follow the road downhill. Although the bus runs this way, the Levada do Curral could be missed on a bendy stretch of road. Walk down the road, and it is easy to spot it flowing downstream to the left, passing above the corrugated roof of a building. The levada path is concrete and passes above vegetable plots, then it turns into a little side valley and is covered by earth and stones. Landslips and rock-falls are common from the cliff of **Pico do Serrado**. After passing through mixed woods, views overlook the main valley from a short stretch of fencing.

Turn round another side valley and proceed without the security of a fence across a steep slope of chestnuts. There are big boulders; some of which came crashing down from the cliff and damaged the path. Chestnuts give way to a small stand of pines and a view of the sheer cliff. Do not loiter, but follow the levada through a little **tunnel**. The channel is covered for a while, and there are valley and peak views before turning a corner into woods again. Chestnut and eucalyptus grow on old cultivation terraces, along with malfurada and prickly pears. Turn round a bare hollow of steep rock, where the levada gushes alongside an uneven path with brambles alongside. After passing a few chestnuts and more thorny scrub, turn a steep-sided rocky gully by negotiating a short, bent **tunnel**.

Turn a corner where there is a sheer drop into the valley, then head into a more vegetated gully, side-stepping a covered stretch of the levada. Continue into eucalyptus, with some mimosa and chestnut, where wet and dripping rock overhangs. Laurel flourishes in a tight little side valley, and the path can be wet and slippery, with the danger of rockfalls. Leave and turn round into the next little side valley, where the path narrows alarmingly and it is not possible to walk beside the levada. Use a wet, crumbling and vegetated path below the levada, then climb up again to continue. Turn a rocky corner with wonderful views of the valley and peaks, then follow a path below the levada again. There is more laurel and a splendid view up the valley.

The Levada do Curral makes a series of descents. A

The Levada do Curral is one of the more frightening levadas on Madeira. It slices southwards from Curral das Freiras, through an impressively steep-sided gorge, clinging to sheer cliffs. The overall descent is around 300m (1000ft). A notoriously difficult stretch occurs at Fajã, where the levada has been hacked from a cliff that continually weeps with water, making everything treacherously slippery. Gates have been erected either side of this stretch and may well be locked, so check in advance if the way is open. The continuation into the suburbs of Funchal is much easier.

Transport:
Camacha Bus 81 serves
Curral das Freiras.
Funchal Bus 16A serves
Pinheiro das Voltas.
Funchal Bus 4, 8, 12 and
48 serve the Caminho de
Esmereldo. Funchal Bus
3, 8, 12, 16, 44 and 48
serve the Caminho de
São Martinho.

Refreshments:
There are shops, bars
and restaurants in Curral
das Freiras, as well as a
couple of bars and a
restaurant in the suburbs
of Funchal.

crumbling path and crude stone steps lead down, with an awesome view of the main valley gorge. The levada drops in the form of a fine waterfall. After being covered for a while, the water chases across the foot of a cliff. Hurry after it and beware of rockfalls, but be careful as the path is uneven, wet and slippery. The levada makes loops across the steep slope and is well vegetated, so you're not really aware of the drop below. Watch for thorny scrub at your feet and overhanging vegetation from above. There is a sheer drop to the bouldery riverbed.

Look across the valley to see the village of Fajã da Galinhas, with terraces dropping steeply to a small hut. There is a significant turn around a rock outcrop. Pass a ruined cottage and old cultivation terraces at Fajã de Dentro. There are a few chestnuts here, then it is mostly laurels again. After some exposed moments and scrubby vegetation the levada makes a sudden downhill rush. Use a stony, crumbling path to stay below the levada, then continue along a rather exposed path. Turn round a corner and walk down exposed steps with care to reach a stand of eucalyptus. There is a view back up the valley to Fajã da Galinhas. Turn another corner, where the levada is covered with rockfall detritus, then a series of descents drop the water level. If the concrete path is wet and slippery, take care on these descents, though the steeper stretches have steps built into them. There are rampant growths of bamboo and brambles on old cultivation terraces at **Fajã**, and one of the old houses is seen as well as a view down through the valley to the sea.

Reach a gateway and hopefully it is not locked; something that should be checked in advance. Pause and study the rather awesome rocky side valley, which is the most dangerous part of the walk. Take great care. Walk down the path and use steps to cross a wedged boulder. Enter a curious **tunnel**, which is quite high and wide, with the water rushing through it. The tunnel is bent, so the exit cannot immediately be seen, but there is a series of 'windows' carved alongside allowing light to enter. A waterfall pours down outside the first of these 'windows' and there are ten more to pass. There are stacks of boul-

Looking over the suburbs of Funchal to the Curral valley and peaks

ders inside the tunnel, and the roof is quite low at the exit. The next stretch is very dangerous. Turn left out of the tunnel, with only a low fence alongside, and walk carefully down 35 steep, exposed and slippery steps. The fence is in tatters and there may be a cable to hold onto for the descent. The levada slices across a cliff face and the overhang continually streams with water. You will get very wet and the parapet is slippery and uneven. Some people prefer to walk along the channel and suffer wet feet rather than risk a fatal slip. It does not take too long to get past this stretch, and although the path beyond is exposed for a while, go through a small rock arch and pass another gateway to reach safer ground.

Take a break and get a few things dried. Take the time to look back into the deeply-cut valley. The deserted houses at Fajã are seen from this stance. There is a mixture of trees and a small vineyard, then the levada has safety fencing. A good path leads through woods and along a cliff, with views from Fajã da Galinhas down to the sea. The levada goes through a rock arch, but the path is on the outside, then turn round a corner. It does not feel exposed with trees growing alongside. Go through a rock cutting and walk along slabs laid over the channel, then turn to look all the way down the Socorridos valley, which is quite industrial. Pass a few houses and the levada is covered as it swings left into another valley.

Bananas dominate the scene and all types of fruit and vegetables grow. The paved stretch of the levada is called the Vereda da Viana, and there are missing and broken slabs. Cross a concrete and iron levada footbridge over the bouldery Ribeira do Arvoredo, where eucalyptus grows. The path is now called the Vereda de Santa Quiteria. Follow it past more houses and cross a steep concrete road. Water is seen in the levada until the next steep road, where it is covered again. Pass vine trellises and bananas, then join and follow a bit of road round into the next valley. The water is seen again on leaving the valley, then join a road and pass a large building, where the levada is buried again. Watch to the right to see it on the Travessa do Tanque. The Bruno **Bar** and bus services are here at Pinheiro das Voltas.

To continue, take the Caminho do Pico do Funcho past the **Bar** Mariano, then turn left along the Vereda da Levada do Poço Barral. This slabbed path passes bananas and crosses a concrete track. Continue along the paved way, passing more bananas and the Recheio Cash and Carry. Emerge on the busy Caminho do Esmereldo, where there are bus services available. Alternatively, use a pedestrian crossing and turn right to reach the O Moinho **restaurant**, then turn left and note the millstone on the corner. The levada is covered at first, but turn right down steps to find it in a concrete aqueduct. Cross the motorway using a curious aqueduct footbridge and continue between a tall wall and more bananas. Descend a flight of steps to the left to reach a road called the Rua do Ninho. Turn right to follow it downhill and it becomes quite narrow. Keep to the right, then turn right at the bottom to reach the busy Caminho de **São Martinho** and buses down into Funchal.

WALK 39: Levada do Piornais

THE ROUTE
Distance:
7 or 12km (4½ or 7½ miles).
Start:
At the bus terminus at Lombada – 163141.
Finish:
Estádio dos Barreiros – 195131.
Maps:
Military Survey 1:25,000 Sheets 8 and 9 or IGC 1:50,000 Madeira East.
Terrain:
The first part, which is optional, is across a steep, rocky, exposed slope and involves negotiating tiny tunnels. The second part is easier and mostly crosses cultivated slopes while moving towards the suburbs of Funchal.

Start on the Caminho da **Lombada**, on a road bend overlooking the lower industrial part of the Socorridos valley and the graceful span of the motorway bridge. Walk uphill from the bus stop, along a narrow road called the Vereda do Pico da Lombada. A short, steep climb leads to a bridge over the motorway, and the **Levada do Piornais** is immediately beyond. Have a look at an information board detailing some of the plants seen along the way. Also note the warnings it gives about heading into the Socorridos valley. On this walk the exposed levada

The Levada do Piornais is one of the oldest levadas on Madeira. Although it has been overhauled many times, it dates from the 15th century, bringing water out of the deep-cut Socorridos valley to moisten sunny slopes around São Martinho. Sugar was once grown extensively, but now bananas cover the slopes. The walk along the Levada do Piornais can be difficult or easy, and there is the option of choosing at the start. Heading into the Socorridos valley, the levada clings to a cliff and passes through tiny tunnels. Walking this way, you have to turn round and retrace steps later. It is a much easier walk in the other direction, towards the suburbs of Funchal.

Transport:
Funchal Bus 1 and 3
serve Lombada. Funchal
Bus 2 and 3 serve
Quebradas. Funchal Bus
2 serves Caminho do
Areeiro. Funchal Bus 4
and 48 serve Caminho
do Amparo. Funchal Bus
45 and 48 serve Estádio
do Barreiros.

Refreshments:
There are small shops
and bars at Quebradas
and Amparo.

leading into the Socorridos valley can be seen first, retracing steps later, otherwise simply follow the easy part of the levada to Funchal.

Heading upstream first for the difficult part of the walk, the levada is covered in concrete and protected by railings. Later, follow a path beside the water, passing plenty of bananas as well as mimosa, a few eucalyptus and pine. Note an arrow pointing down a flight of steps, allowing walkers to descend below a difficult part of the levada and climb up again later. The levada is partly cut into a cliff face and partly supported on stone arches. Anyone choosing to follow the levada will certainly have to crouch, if not actually crawl through a complex gash of a tunnel. There are safety rails, but some walkers would find the exposure unnerving. Space is so limited for walking that slabs have been laid across the watercourse. Continue through another small tunnel then walk across a stone aqueduct arch. Walk on slabs through short rocky cuttings, then cross another arch. A low, fractured tunnel comes next, then walk on slabs across another arch. The levada crosses a stepped concrete path with street lights, and the parapet path leads round into a side valley, passing eucalyptus trees. This stretch is without safety rails and is exposed in places. There are railings across a narrow, single-arched stone bridge over a bouldery gorge, then there are no railings on leaving the valley. Swing round into the main Socorridos valley again, and take care as the level concrete parapet turns into an uneven stone parapet. There is a low tunnel ahead, and a sheer drop below the levada. If you are not already thinking of turning round, then proceed with great care. In any case, go no further than a generating station, which is fed by a pipeline on the opposite side of the valley. Turn round and retrace steps to the information board where the walk started.

Leaving the motorway bridge, the Levada do Piornais is covered in concrete and runs between walls, houses and bananas. The concrete has been renewed, but there are dozens of 'hatches' to trip over. Bananas dominate the scene as virtually the entire slope has been planted. Cross over a road at the head of a valley and continue

Terraces full of bananas are a feature of the Levada do Piornais

on the level. Walk round another little valley drained by a small stream. There is a view back to the mountains, including the summit of Cedro. The levada crosses a road bend then a short stretch leads to a road bridge spanning the motorway. There is a view of the mountains from the bridge, but do not cross over the bridge. Instead, follow the levada a short way alongside the motorway, then climb up to a slip road and follow the Caminho das **Quebradas** in the direction of Funchal. The Bar Restaurante Santa Rita is on this road, as well as a shop called Super das Quebradas. There are also bus services.

Turn right as signposted for Funchal and Areeiro, following the road under the motorway. Turn right down the Caminho das Quebradas de Baixo, then almost immediately left down steps onto the levada. The channel is covered with slabs and there is a tall wall alongside. A house sits on the levada, so drop down a few steps and continue along a cobbled road. When the road rises a little, drop down a couple of steps to the right to continue along the slab-covered channel. Climb up a few steps and cross a road bend on the Caminho do Areeiro. Walk between a wall and a lot of prickly pears, then the slabs finish and water is seen again. There is a wall on one side of the levada and tomatoes and bananas grow down towards the sea. Big hotels and apartments are seen on the western side of Funchal. The levada has street lights, and a flight of steps crosses it on one bend, then another flight of steps forms an arch on another bend. Pass a cave and go under a small stone arch while turning a corner. The tower of São Martinho church is seen on a hill. Take care as the levada parapet is polished stone, then it is concrete again. Cross a busy bend on the Caminho do **Amparo**, where there are bus services and a small shop/bar.

The levada continues between houses, partly covered by slabs and partly open. Cross a minor road and walk along a slabbed section, then follow the open levada by walking along a stone parapet. Looking back, there is a view to the summit tor on Pico Grande. The parapet soon has its own slabs, with a few gaps, and they ring musically when anyone walks along them. Look down on large buildings near the sea, while the Pico da Ponta da Cruz rising above is completely covered with prickly pears and crowned with masts. While following another slabbed stretch, there are views of the Ilhas Desertas, as well as the built-up southernmost point of Madeira at Ponta da Cruz.

The levada drops down a little and there is an old millstone before a walk through a flowery cutting. The concrete parapet leads round a slope and offers views over Funchal and its harbour. The levada is again covered in slabs for a short way before it crosses a road. Continue along a slabbed stretch and an open stretch, then walk alongside a busy road. Steps lead up onto this road close to the **stadium** called Estádio dos Barreiros. There are bus services, but you are not too far from the centre of **Funchal** if you want to walk down into town.

WALK 40: Levada da Negra

THE ROUTE
Distance:
8km (5 miles).
Start:
Poço da Neve on the Pico do Areeiro road – 200222.
Finish:
At the bus terminus at Barreira – 176175.
Maps:
Military Survey 1:25,000 Sheets 5, 6 and 8 or IGC
1:50,000 Madeira East.
Terrain:
Essentially a mountain walk with some steep and rocky
slopes. The levada path is narrow and stony in places,
with some short exposed stretches. The final parts are
well wooded.

The Levada da Negra is a fine mountain levada. Its narrow channel carries water at speed from the southern flanks of Pico do Areeiro and Cedro to Funchal. Start on the road from Poiso to Pico do Areeiro, and maybe even visit the summit of Areeiro first for early morning views. The walk starts at the Poço da Neve ice house beside the mountain road. Cross a rugged valley to link with the Levada da Negra, then follow it downstream. It descends steeply and traverses the rocky Santo António valley. There is a wooded slope before the walk finishes at Barreira high above Funchal.

Start at **Poço da Neve** on the road from Poiso to Pico do Areeiro. There is a small signpost at a gate beside the road and a path leads down to the stone igloo-shaped ice house. Ice was stored in a deep pit during the winter, then cut and transported at speed down to Funchal through the summer. This was not just to cool drinks and desserts, but also for medical use. Start at an altitude of 1650m (5415ft) and basically walk down to Funchal, though you will discover that the way is often rough and stony.

A grassy path runs downhill from the ice house, crossing a track and continuing down a slope of grass and bracken, with some boulders dotted about. Reach another grassy path and turn right to follow it across the slope. It becomes a stony track leading to a gate beside a river. Cross the bouldery riverbed and climb up the track to reach the Levada da Negra as it flows across a broad gap. Take in the view to Pico do Areeiro at the head of

The Levada da Negra crosses a gap and flows vigorously downhill

the valley, as it will not be seen again on this walk. Instead, the next big mountain in view is Cedro. Follow the levada downstream. It is a remarkably narrow channel surrounded by close-cropped grass and boulders. It leads in a straight line across the gap and picks up speed as it descends more and more steeply. There are stone steps alongside on the steepest parts. Look to the right to see rounded stone structures; some of them surmounted by domed frames. These are **ice houses** similar to Poço da Neve, but in ruins.

Follow the levada, sometimes using a steep, worn and broken path. Watch out for little feeder channels. The levada suddenly pours as a waterfall, past a fine example of tree heather, into the bouldery bed of the **Ribeira de Santo António de Madalena**. Rather than flowing down the river, the water flows to the other side and continues along the Levada da Negra. The levada is less steeply inclined and slices across the valley side. The valley itself, however, falls quite impressively, featuring rocky gorges and deep rock pools. When there is a good flow of water there are several fine waterfalls.

Turn round a corner for a view along the valley to the sea and spot Funchal. The path stays close to the levada, but when a rocky, bouldery gully is reached, the path runs a little below the flow. Heather grows on the rock above and below the levada, then there is a stretch where the channel drops more steeply with steps. Note other little channels supplementing the flow. Drop below the levada again where it cuts into another rocky gully, and the stepped path continues down as the levada flows more steeply. There is a level stretch passing a few pines on a steep slope. There was once a fire here, and charred trunks lie scattered around. Heather now colonises the slopes, and there is a huddle of chestnuts beside the bouldery river.

The water picks up speed again for another short downhill run, levelling out again after turning a corner. Although the slope is very steep and rocky, the path is wide and well buttressed. Although stony and uneven in places, some parts of the path are almost level and covered in short grass. After another descent with steps, make a curious tight little turn, then continue more or less on the level. Take the time to look back up through the valley, then go through a gate into eucalyptus and lose the views. There is a narrow path beside the levada, leading to a small concrete hut where another levada slices straight across. Be sure to swing sharply right to continue following the Levada da Negra downstream.

Continue through eucalyptus woods, and notice a few tall, charred pines. Swing in and out of a little valley, then walk down into another little valley, making a tight turn to exit. A broader path describes gentler curves round the slope, passing eucalyptus, pines and tall chestnuts. A path runs downhill to reach a broad, stone-paved road. Turn left to follow this downhill, along a crest with sparse tree cover. Levadas flow on both sides of the road. Walk past a farm, then there are street lights and tall trees while continuing down to a water building. Walk down a steep concrete road with steps down the middle. When you land at a tarmac turning space at **Barreira**, there is a bus stop immediately alongside, where the next bus can be taken down into **Funchal**.

Transport:
Nova minibuses use the Pico do Areeiro road, otherwise use a taxi. Funchal Bus 10 serves Barreira.

Refreshments:
None, but the bus into Funchal passes several bars at the end.

WALK 41: Levada do Barreiro

The Levada do Barreiro offers a good route down from the Pico do Areeiro road to Monte. Start walking at the Poço da Neve ice house on the mountain road. The route downhill is almost entirely confined to the Parque Ecológico do Funchal. This area is gradually having some of its original tree cover re-established, is the subject of ongoing studies, and is popular with school parties. The Levada do Barreiro is narrow and sometimes descends steeply across rugged slopes and rock faces. For the most part it is well wooded, though there are open slopes and good views. On reaching the lower roads, simply continue down to Monte to finish.

THE ROUTE

Distance:
9km (5½ miles).

Start:
Poço da Neve on the Pico do Areeiro road – 200222.

Finish:
At the square at Monte – 219167.

Maps:
Military Survey 1:25,000 Sheets 5, 6 and 8 or IGC 1:50,000 Madeira East.

Terrain:
Paths can be vague at first, and quite rugged and slippery later. Some wooded slopes are quite overgrown. The route ends with an old road.

Start at **Poço da Neve** on the road from Poiso to Pico do Areeiro. There is a small signpost at a gate beside the road and a path leads down to the stone igloo-shaped ice house. Ice was stored in a deep pit during the winter, then cut and transported at speed down to Funchal through the summer. This was not just to cool drinks and desserts, but also for medical use. Start at an altitude of 1650m (5415ft) and basically walk down to Monte, though you will discover that the way is often rough and stony.

A grassy path runs downhill from the ice house, crossing a track and continuing down a slope of grass and bracken, with some boulders dotted about. Keep well to the right of a large patch of tree heather. Cross another grassy path and a stony track, then pick a way down towards a stand of pines, aiming to the left of them. Cross a little valley drained by a small stream, and a signpost points left along the Levada Afluente. Follow the levada round a corner, passing a solitary, gnarled specimen of tree heather. The channel descends past a few tall pines, then drops over a rocky lip and rushes down to a stream in a valley. Do not follow it all the way, but watch carefully for another levada, usually without water, off to the right. This leads across a slope of tree heather and down to the river.

Cross the bouldery riverbed and take care following the levada onwards. The water sometimes flows through a black plastic pipe, which may be buried, but is occasionally seen on the surface. A vague path traces its course, leading through tree heather and across a steep and stony slope. Drop down towards the river later, and be sure to spot the levada channel, where a sign points back up to Poço da Neve. A much better path runs alongside the **Levada do Barreiro**, cutting through tree heather. Pass a signposted junction where another path climbs uphill, but keep following the levada, as marked for Casa do Barreiro. The path swings round to cross a stream, then picks its way across another slope covered in tree heather. There are fine views across the Santa Luzia valley, as well as a view of a waterfall.

The path steepens and the levada has fencing alongside where the slope is more exposed or slippery. Take care at these points. The levada leads through dense woodlands of pine, mimosa, holm oak and tree heather. The path is vague and rugged at times and there is matted undergrowth in places. There are some open slopes and views across the valley or down towards Funchal. If the walking proves too difficult, look out for a signpost pointing left for the Estrada Florestal, which is a loop of forest road offering easy walking towards Poiso.

Keep walking steeply down the ridge, taking care as the path is rough and narrow. Cross a track and walk down a narrower and more overgrown path. Land on the track further down, where signposts point back uphill for the Levada do Barreiro and Poço da Neve. Turn left to follow the track round the valley to pass white buildings at **Casa do Barreiro**. The track leads through green gates to leave the Parque Ecológico do Funchal, and a tarmac road leads onwards. Cross a slope of tall eucalyptus and

Transport:
Nova minibuses use the Pico do Areeiro road, otherwise use a taxi. Funchal Bus 20, 21 and 48 serve Monte. Taxis at Monte.

Refreshments:
The Snack Bar Alto Monte and Café do Parque are at Monte.

The Poço da Neve Ice House is high on the road to Pico do Areeiro

pine, then pass a quarry on the left, and a house on the right. The road leads to a junction with the ER-202 on a hairpin bend. Follow the main road downhill to reach the next hairpin bend where a sign announces **Terreiro da Luta**, with a signpost pointing left for Monte.

Walk down a cobbled track, passing a notice explaining how Our Lady of Monte appeared in a vision to a young shepherd girl. There is a statue higher up the slope and there was once a funicular railway between Funchal and Terreiro da Luta. The cobbled track leads downhill on a steep slope of pines, with mimosa and gorse growing alongside. There are street lights alongside and a little levada carries water. After making a couple of bends, reach some houses and turn right. The old road continues downhill as a patchy tarmac and cobbled affair, passing more houses. It is called the Caminho do Monte and when it reaches a junction with another road go down a flight of steps to reach the square at **Monte**. A cobbled square is used as a car park and taxi rank. Tall plane trees offer shade and stalls sell souvenirs. The Snack Bar Alto Monte and Café do Parque are located here, with toilets in between. There are buses running down into **Funchal**.

WALK 42: Levada do Caldeirão Verde

THE ROUTE

Distance:
17 or 21km (10½ or 13 miles) there and back.
Start/Finish:
Pico das Pedras – 229281 or Queimadas – 218285.
Maps:
Military Survey 1:25,000 Sheets 5 and 6 or
IGC 1:50,000 Madeira East.
Terrain:
The levada path is easy and well wooded at the start.
There are eight tunnels and several narrow, rugged
paths to follow later. Some paths can be a little exposed
and rather slippery.

This walk can be started at Pico das Pedras or
Queimadas. There are no bus services to these points,
but taxis can be hired in Santana. Consequently, the finish
can be at Queimadas or Pico das Pedras later in the day.
Starting at **Pico das Pedras**, leave the road as if visiting
the Orancho Restaurant, but walk between the restaurant
and a chalet development, along a narrow road with
stone gateposts. A winding track continues through mixed
woodlands, though there is a predominance of eucalyptus. The track is alongside the **Levada do Caldeirão
Verde**, though at a rock cutting the track goes straight
through while the levada turns round a spur. There are
places where the looping levada is covered in stone slabs,
and sometimes there are gaps, so watch your feet. After
turning round a couple of little valleys, cross a river
where there are stone picnic tables and follow the levada
to **Queimadas.**

The Parque das Queimadas has a small cobbled car
park and a cobbled path leads past a couple of attractive

The Levada do
Caldeirão Verde can be
as easy or as difficult as
walkers want it to be.
The first stages are
delightfully easy and
richly wooded, and
there is a choice of two
starting points. As
progress is made along
the levada, there are
several tunnels and
plenty of narrow paths.
On reaching Caldeirão
Verde, either turn
around at that point or
continue further into a
steep-sided and well-
wooded valley.
Climbing up a rugged
slope to a higher
levada, it is possible to
walk to Caldeirão do
Inferno, where
waterfalls pour into a
deep, dark gorge.

185

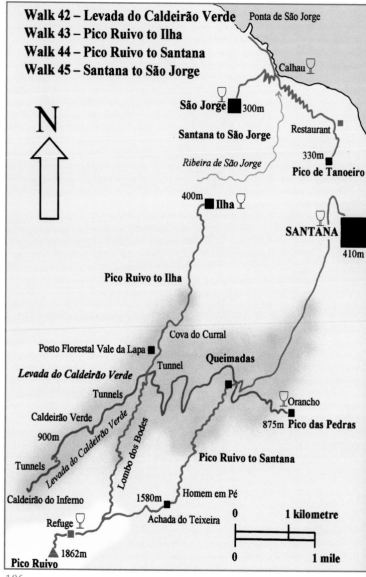

Walk 42 – Levada do Caldeirão Verde
Walk 43 – Pico Ruivo to Ilha
Walk 44 – Pico Ruivo to Santana
Walk 45 – Santana to São Jorge

Ponta de São Jorge

N

Calhau

São Jorge 300m

Santana to São Jorge

Restaurant

Ribeira de São Jorge

330m
Pico de Tanoeiro

400m Ilha

SANTANA
410m

Pico Ruivo to Ilha

Cova do Curral

Posto Florestal Vale da Lapa

Levada do Caldeirão Verde

Tunnel

Queimadas

Tunnels

Levada do Caldeirão Verde

Orancho

Caldeirão Verde

Lombo dos Bodes

875m Pico das Pedras

900m

Tunnels

Pico Ruivo to Santana

Caldeirão do Inferno

1580m Homem em Pé

Refuge

Achada do Teixeira

Pico Ruivo 1862m

0   1 kilometre

0   1 mile

thatched houses. The path is signposted for Caldeirão Verde and Caldeirão do Inferno, passing through a picnic area among tall trees, then crossing a small duckpond. The levada is again signposted and a broad and clear path continues with tall trees alongside. Cross over a track and note how hydrangeas and oaks grow beside the levada, through the slopes are covered in 'laurisilva'. Go through a gate and a narrower path leads onwards. There are views of wooded ridges and valleys, while in the distance the Posto Florestal Vale da Lapa can be seen.

The path has some fencing, but is not particularly exposed. There are some dripping and slippery stretches, and steps lead across a stream below a waterfall at Corrego Queimadas. Leave the valley and there is more fencing alongside the path on the way round to the next valley. Cross a levada bridge at the head of the valley, but note how the levada once went further into the deep, green gorge. The path continues with more fencing, making a pronounced turn into the next valley. Pass through a small rock cutting on a densely wooded slope of laurel and tree heather. There are views from time to time, taking in a slender waterfall and peaks high above. Cross a concrete bridge to face the waterfall, which cascades across the levada. Leave the valley and continue along the partly-fenced path. There is a view down the valley for a while, but also plenty of vegetation, with tree heather leaning low across the path. Watch for rock cuttings with low headroom. The path winds across a slope and a couple of parts are covered in landslip debris. Go through a low, bendy **tunnel** with an uneven path, then continue across a slope of tree heather and laurel. There is a signpost for Caldeirão Verde pointing straight through another tunnel.

A torch is required. The **tunnel** is high and the path is broad, with the narrow levada being followed upstream. There is a fence inside the tunnel. The path becomes uneven, the roof lowers, and there is a wall between the path and the water. Exit with a fine view of a deep valley before the next tunnel. There is a fairly high wall between the path and the levada in the **tunnel**, and there is low headroom and rather constricted spaces. The

A view down the deep and steep-sided valley near Caldeirão do Inferno

path is narrow, uneven and wet, with a 'window' offering a view of the valley alongside. The tunnel is quite bendy, though the exit is higher and drier. The path is fenced, though not too exposed, but the parapet is broken and needs care. A narrow part of the parapet is avoided by switching to steps down and up. The path is partly fenced as it winds across a steep slope to the next tunnel. Slabs cover part of the levada, and the **tunnel** is short and curved. Continue across long and steep slopes and cliffs, well-vegetated in places, and more exposed in others. A pronounced turn leads into a huge green gully, where there is an orange sign. This is **Caldeirão Verde**.

If the path so far has been rough enough, then note that it gets rougher further along, so some walkers may wish to turn back at this point. The continuation is signposted for Caldeirão do Inferno, picking its way across a fenced slope to leave the green gully. Turn round beside a big stump of rock to rejoin the main valley. Continue across a slope without fencing, then with tattered fencing. There are steps down from the levada at a narrow cut, crossing a scree slope with steps up on the other side. After passing tall til trees, watch for an eroded flight of steps up to the left. There are about 200 steps here, though there may once have been twice that number. Take care as the slope is steep and rugged. Reach a higher levada at a junction of three tunnels. Do not go through the one on the left, except maybe for a view. The one straight ahead has railway lines and leads under Pico Ruivo to the Central de Noguiera generating station. Turn right through the shortest **tunnel** and pass a wide, deep tank to continue.

Walk along an uneven and exposed path. A waterfall pours down into front of another short **tunnel**. Go through and then immediately turn round into the next **tunnel**. This is a long and bendy tunnel with a good path and headroom. Later, there is plenty of headroom, but the path is wet. It is rather lower and the path is stony on the way out of the tunnel. Walk along an even, but unfenced parapet and take care if it is wet and slippery. The last **tunnel** is bendy and rumbles ominously. Use a torch as there is a stony path and low headroom. Although the exit cannot be seen at first, there are four 'windows' looking out into a deep, dark, green and narrow gorge. The rumbling noise becomes louder. Climb out of the tunnel to find two waterfalls thundering down into the gorge at **Caldeirão do Inferno**. Admire them, but obviously there is no way out of this place except by retracing your steps. Return to Queimadas or Pico das Pedras to finish the walk, though it is also possible to cut off to Ilha or Santana by referring to Walk 43 or Walk 44.

Transport:
Taxi to and from Pico das Pedras or Queimadas.

Refreshments:
Orancho Restaurante at Pico das Pedras.

WALK 43: Pico Ruivo to Ilha

Most of the signposts between Ilha and Pico Ruivo point uphill, as if this route was intended primarily as an ascent route. That would be difficult on a hot and humid day, but as a descent route it is obviously easier. The higher parts of the path are waymarked, but are not too clear. Following a ridge down through tree heather, however, the way is much clearer. Crossing the Levada do Caldeirão Verde, further explorations could be made to right or left. The way to Ilha seems to level out, but there are still some steep and deeply worn paths before the village is finally reached.

THE ROUTE

Distance:
10km (6 miles).

Start:
The summit of Pico Ruivo – 184258.

Finish:
At the church in Ilha – 213315.

Maps:
Military Survey 1:25,000 Sheets 3, 5 and 6 or IGC 1:50,000 Madeira East.

Terrain:
Mountainous. The path down from Pico Ruivo is clear, easy and paved. The spur to Ilha is vague and rugged at the top, but clearer as it descends a wooded ridge. An old levada and steep, deeply-cut paths lead finally to Ilha.

Start on the summit of **Pico Ruivo**, where there is a large trig point at 1862m (6109ft) and a monument. The summit is surrounded by a wooden fence and is a fine viewpoint. Look back along the rugged ridge to Pico do Areeiro, as well as down into the deep valley towards Curral das Freiras. Pico Grande is identified by its prominent summit tor, then look along the rugged crest of Madeira towards the plateau of Paúl da Serra. Densely wooded slopes fall away to the north coast and the path heading eastwards to Teixeira can be seen. Walk downhill and turn right at a path junction to reach the **refuge**.

Leave the refuge and walk down steps to reach a path junction, then turn left down a paved path, crossing an area of bare pumice. More steps lead down through tree heather and through a gate. Walk past big boulders and rocky outcrops, where there are views off to the right of the rugged ridge leading to Pico do Areeiro. The path passes a stone shelter and switches to the other side of the ridge, then a signpost points down to the left for Ilha. The path is vague, but is marked with red and yellow paint flashes. Cross a water pipe and note that the path is a ribbon of green grass, with crude steps, and the slope is liberally scattered with stones. Follow the path across a steep and rugged slope, generally descending, with good views all round. Notice how other mountain ridges drop steeply, but the path heads for the **Lombo dos Bodes**, which is a gentler ridge.

There are some rocky outcrops on the crest of the ridge, but the path slips off to the left side, passing a rock-face, then switches to the right and heads down into tree heather on a lower part of the ridge. There are still good views and the path is good too, with plenty of earth steps. Reach a path junction in denser tree heather, where a signpost points back to Pico Ruivo and left for Semagral, but keep walking downhill. There are good views across Caldeirão Verde and Caldeirão do Inferno, as well as the mountains around the valleys. The path swings right and drops down through a deep rut where the ground is mossy and slippery. Take care while continuing down-hill, passing a few little caves. Views are limited. There is a pronounced bend steeply down to the left, and tree heather gives way to til trees. Watch for a gap on the left, where there is a fine view, then continue down the path, which levels out at a junction. Straight ahead is sign-posted for the Posto Florestal Vale da Lapa, but turn sharply right and left to walk down to another junction, quite close to a point where the **Levada do Caldeirão Verde** goes into a tunnel.

A detour could be made to look at the levada, or even follow its course by referring to Walk 42, but to reach Ilha, turn left at the junction as signposted. Follow the course of an old levada across a slope of laurel and heather, where some rock outcrops have a bit of fencing. There are hydrangeas alongside, but the water in the levada flows through a black plastic pipe, if it is seen at all. The path drops downhill, though there is a detour up to a spring also available. Go through a gate, rejoining the path from the **Posto Florestal Vale da Lapa**. Continue down worn stone steps on the other side of the ridge,

Transport:
São Roque Bus 103 and 138 serve Ilha.

Refreshments:
There is a small bar at the refuge on Pico Ruivo, and small shops and bars at Ilha.

Rainbow over Caldeirão Verde on the descent from Pico Ruivo

generally in mixed woods, to reach a turning point at the end of a track. A signpost points back to Pico Ruivo, and take care as the track surface can be slippery.

Follow the track for a while, but when a right bend is reached, walk straight on along a grassy crest. A path drops down steps in a deep cutting to reach a track at a lower level. Cross over the track and continue along another grassy crest, then follow the path into another deeper and darker cutting. At the next track, turn right downhill, then left along another track as signposted for Ilha. Walk straight along a cultivated crest to reach some huts. A signpost for Garnal points left down steps across cultivated slopes. Go through another deep and dark cutting to land on another track. Cross the track and keep to the right of a circular tank to find a path leading down past more plots. Flights of concrete steps lead down past a house to land on a road. Turn left to follow the road down to the church at **Ilha**. The bus turns here and there are a couple of small shops and bars nearby.

WALK 44: Pico Ruivo to Santana

THE ROUTE

Distance:

11.5km (7 miles).

Start:

The summit of Pico Ruivo – 184258.

Finish:

In the middle of Santana – 243309.

Maps:

Military Survey 1:25,000 Sheets 3, 5 and 6 or IGC 1:50,000 Madeira East.

Terrain:

Mountainous. The path down from Pico Ruivo is clear, easy and paved. The wooded descent to Queimadas can be steep and slippery. The final descent to Santana is along an easy road.

Start on the summit of **Pico Ruivo**, where there is a large trig point at 1862m (6109ft) and a monument. The summit is surrounded by a wooden fence and is a fine viewpoint. Look back along the rugged ridge to Pico do Areeiro, as well as down into the deep valley towards Curral das Freiras. Pico Grande is identified by its prominent summit tor, then look along the rugged crest of Madeira towards the plateau of Paúl da Serra. Densely wooded slopes fall away to the north coast and the path heading eastwards to Teixeira can be seen. Walk downhill and turn right at a path junction to reach the **refuge**.

Leave the refuge and walk down steps to reach a path junction, then turn left down a paved path, crossing an area of bare pumice. More steps lead down through tree heather and through a gate. Walk past big boulders and rocky outcrops, where there are views off to the right of the rugged ridge leading to Pico do Arèeiro. The path passes a stone shelter and switches to the other side of the ridge then a signpost points ahead to Achada do

This is quite a long descent from Pico Ruivo, though it could be considered in three separate parts. First there is a fairly easy walk down from the summit to the car park at Achada do Teixeira. Second is a path crossing the road at a lower level, zig-zagging steeply down through heather and laurel to Queimadas on the Levada do Caldeirão Verde. All that remains from that point is a simple walk down a rugged road to complete the descent to Santana. Arrange to be collected at Queimadas to finish early, or follow a stretch of the Levada do Caldeirão Verde to extend the walk.

193

Transport:

Taxi to or from Achada
do Teixeira or
Queimadas. São Roque
Bus 103 and 138 serve
Santana. Taxis at
Santana.

Refreshments:

There is a small bar at
the refuge on Pico Ruivo,
and a number of shops,
bars and restaurants
around Santana.

Teixeira. The paved path climbs, then descends and passes another stone shelter and picnic tables, where there is also a water source. Follow the path up, along and down to another stone shelter, then walk along the broad ridge for a while. Go down through a fence and zig-zag down to the car park and building at **Achada do Teixeira**. The altitude is around 1580m (5185ft). Spend a while looking over into the Metade valley and along the array of jagged peaks leading to Pico do Areeiro. Sometimes there are taxis waiting in the car park, while their clients walk to Pico Ruivo and back. They might be willing to run walkers to Santana.

To continue the descent, walk in front of the building, between fenced areas that are regenerating their vegetation, and turn left downhill. Walk through a gap in a wall and fencing, into a shallow valley where there are a few huts. Keep to the right of a peculiar, block-shaped, leaning outcrop called **Homem em Pé**. Walk down a grassy path to a hut, then just below the hut, turn left and roughly contour across a slope of tall heather. The path runs down a ridge and leads onto a series of narrow zig-zags down through tall heather. Be careful at the end of the path when stepping down onto a road bend. To the right are picnic tables, while to the left are steps leading down from the road.

Walk down these crude steps, where eroded stretches can be steep and slippery. The descent is not recommended in wet weather. The path is often a deeply-cut rut flanked by tree heather, while zig-zags seem to go on forever. When other tree species begin to appear, alongside a steep paved track, reach a gate and pass through. There is dense 'laurisilva', then a few open spaces at a couple of houses. Continue down to a car park and take a peek to the left at a couple of lovely thatched houses at **Queimadas**. The Levada do Caldeirão Verde is crossed at this point, signposted to left and right, and can be followed by referring to Walk 42.

Arrange to be collected at Queimadas to save the last 5km (3 miles) of road-walking down to Santana. Queimadas is at an altitude of 883m (2897ft) and the road leaving the car park turns right and begins its steep

Looking beyond the mountain refuge on Pico Ruivo towards the sea

descent. It runs more gently around and across a bouldery stream, and is flanked by laurels and hydrangeas. The road is a patchy affair of cobbles and tarmac. It rises a little and runs through eucalyptus, then descends again in mixed woodlands. After passing a circular tank there is another fairly level stretch, then it descends more steeply, passing eucalyptus, pine and mimosa. A lower stretch is concrete, leading to a junction with a tarmac road, where the route runs straight ahead. Turn right and right again at junctions, then cross the main ER-101 road before walking down into the middle of **Santana**. There are places to eat and drink in the village, as well as toilets and a bus stop. There are several little thatched houses, some of them in the classic red and white 'Santana' style colours.

WALK 45: Santana to São Jorge

Santana and São Jorge sit on elevated slopes high above the sea. Between them is a deep valley drained by the Ribeira de São Jorge, carrying water from Pico Ruivo to the sea. The modern main road loops and zig-zags from one village to the other, but in the past people followed a more direct cobbled road. It still exists and offers a fine walking route, reaching the sea at the tiny settlement of Calhau. A diversion is recommended at that point, following another path along the cliff coast to the rugged Ponta de São Jorge. Other notable coastal viewpoints nearby include the Rocha do Navio, with its little cablecar service near Santana, and Vigia near São Jorge.

THE ROUTE

Distance:
6.5km (4 miles).
Start:
Pico de Tanoeiro near Santana – 237323.
Finish:
At the church in São Jorge – 218334.
Maps:
Military Survey 1:25,000 Sheet 3 or
IGC 1:50,000 Madeira East.
Terrain:
Mostly along winding cobbled tracks on steep slopes.

Start near **Santana**, where there is a bus stop and small shop at **Pico de Tanoeiro**. Walk away from the main ER-101 road by following a patchy cobbled and tarmac road uphill. The road levels out, passes a few houses, and reaches an old ruined pink building. Keep to the right to pass below it and the patchy road becomes a rugged track, zig-zagging down to a tarmac road. There are fine views of the hotel and **restaurant** at Quinta do Furão, with orderly rows of vines and vegetable plots surrounding it. Turn left along the road and immediately turn right at a junction. Follow the road along and gently uphill, watching for a sign on the left for São Jorge and Calhau.

Pass a couple of houses while walking downhill then follow a grassy, cobbled old track down past plots and terraces. Later this old road is quite broad and zig-zags on a well-engineered course down what is almost a cliff face. Pico Ruivo rises high above the head of the valley, and prickly pears grow on the lower slopes. Cross an arched bridge over the Ribeira de São Jorge. A car park lies at a road-end to the left, but turn right to walk through the little seaside settlement of **Calhau**. There is access to he pebbly beach and river-mouth, otherwise walk past the few buildings along the track, which include Neptunos night-club and the Bar Disco Calhau. Both places are usually closed during the day. Further up the track there is a junction alongside the last inhabited house and some ruins.

There is a splendid cliff-coast path available by walking straight onwards. A cobbled track and path slice across the cliff face, rising and falling gently. Beware of rockfalls as the cliff occasionally sheds huge boulders. One stretch of path is well-buttressed, then stone steps lead up an old landslip. Continue along the path and turn round a corner to see the rocky **Ponta de São Jorge**, with fishermen's huts perched precariously over deep water. The end of the path has collapsed, and fishermen have to scramble down to the beach, climb a knotted rope, walk along exposed staging and climb a ladder to reach their huts. Walkers probably will not wish to follow them, so turn round and walk back along the cliff path to return to Calhau.

When the junction of cobbled tracks is reached at **Calhau**, turn right and start the zig-zag ascent, passing a few plots and terraces. There are wild tangles of vegetation, as well as an undercut cliff where the track has been hacked from the rock. Tall pines and eucalyptus grow at the top of the slope, and they have been burnt in the past. Reach a cobbled car park and picnic site, where there is an old winch that used to serve Calhau. Do not walk up the road from the car park, but follow another winding cobbled track up a slope covered in pines to reach a walled graveyard. Follow the road away, which is the Rua São Pedro, to reach a junction with another road beside a chapel. Walk straight along the Rua Dr Leonel Mendonça into **São Jorge**. The church contains some extravagant gilded carvings and is well worth a visit. Toilets and bus stops are just down the road, and there are a few snack bars and restaurants. Note the typical style of the old houses in the area, which are wooden with thatched roofs.

Transport:
São Roque Bus 103 and 138 serve Santana and São Jorge. Taxis at Santana.

Refreshments:
Restaurant at Quinta do Furão. Nightclub and Disco Bar (usually closed) at Calhau. There are a few bars and restaurants at São Jorge.

The zig-zag track used
for the descent to the
valley bottom at Calhau

WALK 46: Poiso to Santana

THE ROUTE

Distance:
20km (12½ miles).

Start:
Casa de Abrigo do Poiso – 234206.

Finish:
In the middle of Santana – 243309.

Maps:
Military Survey 1:25,000 Sheets 3 and 6 or IGC
1:50,000 Madeira East.

Terrain:
Wooded and cultivated valleys, with steep paths, tracks
and roads.

Start high on the ER-103 road at the Casa de Abrigo do **Poiso** Restaurante. The altitude of the road pass is 1412m (4633ft). Walk through a junction planted with flowers and shrubs, signposted for Ribeiro Frio. As the road begins its descent, turn left down a grassy cobbled track. This is the old road, flanked by tall pines yet still offering fine views of the high peaks. Simply walk down the cobbled track, straight through a junction with another track, then continue straight across the main road. A broad dirt road, that can be muddy in wet weather, leads to an unsightly dump, the Vazadouro do Terras. Walk straight through, between mounds of earth, and the cobbled road reappears on the other side. It runs down through tree heather and out onto a level area used for sheep grazing. Pass a huddle of buildings and sheep pens at **Chão das Feiteiras** and continue along a close-cropped grassy track. There are splendid views of the high peaks from Pico do Areeiro to Torres, Pico Ruivo and Achada do Teixeira.

The bus from Funchal to Santana loops around wooded ridges and steep-sided valleys. The roads are often steep and zig-zagging, but they were steeper and zig-zagged more in the past. Rediscover the old road to Santana by following it from its highest point at Poiso. It crosses a series of valleys, so expect some climbing along the way, as well as road walking where the old road is buried beneath tarmac. Start early and you can take your time, but if an early finish is needed then the walk crosses the bus route in places. The old road is broad, cobbled and often some distance from the modern road.

SANTANA
410m

ATLANTIC OCEAN

FAIAL

Restaurant

Penha de Águia

690m   Cova da Roda

Penha de Águia
▲ 589m

430m   Lombo Galego

Ribeira de São Roque do Faial

Cruz   240m

PORTO DA CRUZ

Poiso to Santana

Fajã da Murta   300m

420m ■ Cruzinhas

Cabeço do Rochau

N

Carvalho

▲ Pedreiro
792m

**Pico do Suna &
Porto da Cruz**

ER-103 Road   Cabeço Furado   Pico do Suna

900m
■ Ribeiro Frio

▲
1028m

0   1 kilometre

Lombo Comprido

Chão das Feiteiras

0   1 mile

**Walk 46 – Poiso to Santana
Walk 47 – Pico do Suna &
Porto da Cruz
Walk 48 – Penha de Águia**

ER-202 Road
130m
■ Poiso 1412m   Cabeço Gordo

When the track bends right, turn sharply left instead, and walk downhill through a gate into dense tree heather. The cobbled road continues steeply downhill, grassy in its upper parts, then with rolled steps as it turns round a series of bends. There are a few laurels among the heather as the old road drops down to the main road, and a few stone steps complete the descent. Turn right and follow the main road round a rocky bend to reach a parking space on the left. An obvious track descends through more mixed woodlands and the rolled steps are grassy or mossy, winding further down to the road. Water is aerated in a curious stepped levada and flows downstream from a picnic site to a trout farm at the Posto Aquicola do Ribeiro Frio. There is a bar to the left and the Restaurante Ribeiro Frio to the right of the road.

The old road is buried beneath the main road all the way down through the straggly village of **Ribeiro Frio**. It is possible to use part of the path leading in the direction of Balcões to omit part of the road walk. If you choose this then refer to Walk 8, otherwise walk down the road, passing the Restaurante Refugio do Vale and another small bar. The road rises gently beyond the village and there are good views of the valley. There is plenty of mimosa growing above the road and a fine view back to Pico do Areeiro. Pass a picnic site on a bend, then follow the road down past a bus shelter. Off to the left is a road signposted as the Caminho Municipal da Achada do Cedro Gordo. Walk down this bendy concrete road for a sudden view of the high peaks. The vegetation flanking the road is often wild and tangled, but all kinds of fruit and vegetables are grown in small plots around **Carvalho**. Reach a road bend where there is a church and shop/bar on the left.

Walk a short way down the main road, then turn left along a cobbled track that is quite grassy at first. This is the old road again, and take care when it develops steep and slippery zig-zags on a steep and well-wooded slope. Walk down to the main road again and simply cross over to continue down a slope planted with vines. Turn right down a concrete road, but leave this by dropping down to the right to follow a stony track down to a bridge. This

Transport:
São Roque Bus 56, 103 and 138 serve Poiso, Ribeiro Frio and Cruzinhas. São Roque Bus 103 and 138 serve Santana. Taxis at Santana.

Refreshments:
There are bar/restaurants at Poiso and Ribeiro Frio. There are more shops, bars and restaurants around Santana.

substantial stone-arched bridge spans the bouldery Ribeira da Metade and there is a fine house alongside. Zig-zag up the other side of the valley on a narrowing track, looking down through the valley past the houses to the rugged hill of Penha de Águia. Cross a narrow tarmac road and continue up a concrete path to reach the main road, turning right to follow it to a road junction in the tiny village of **Cruzinhas**.

A road at Cruzinhas is signposted for Fajã da Murta, but it zig-zags all over the valley side. The old road is more direct, running below the new road buttress as a steep concrete road with steps down the middle. It has its own street lights and drops well below the zig-zag road, changing to grassy steps as it drops further into the valley. Pass below another buttress on a road bend, then cross over the tarmac road. Go down steps on the other side and the path continues, finally swinging left to land on the road almost in the bottom of the valley. Follow the road down around a bend, then either cross the road bridge, or turn right just beforehand and cross an old footbridge hidden among a few houses. The river is the Ribeira Seca, and at the head of the valley, Pico do Areeiro is seen one last time on this walk.

Follow the road up through **Fajã da Murta**, round a bend and across a bridge. Turn round another bend, but do not follow the road across another bridge. Instead, climb up steps with street lights alongside and cross a little river in a steep side valley, then continue up a stony track. Climb in zig-zags with a view of Penha de Águia, and the slopes are well cultivated and dotted with houses. Swing round into a higher side valley and follow a concrete road as it rises and falls, passing a number of houses and farms. After crossing the Ribeira do Lombo Galego at an old bridge and building, a more patchy road climbs up to a junction with a tarmac road at **Lombo Galego**. Turn left up a concrete road, always zig-zagging uphill on the clearest route. After passing the last house, the concrete runs out, so follow a broad, cobbled track again. There are a couple of bits of concrete, with cultivation terraces and storage huts on the slopes, then views are lost as the track swings left round a corner into a valley full of eucalyptus. The track is grassy and it runs

Classic thatched red and white houses can be seen around Santana

down to an old bridge over the Ribeira da Albelheira.

Zig-zag uphill from the bridge, climbing along the grassy track, and keep to the right at an intersection with another track. Reach a well-signposted crossroads at **Cova da Roda**, and walk straight through as indicated for Santana. Other destinations include Pico das Pedras, Cruzinhas, Faial, Lombo Galego and Cortado. The track passes a building and water tank, and there is a large area to the right under cultivation. Follow the cobbled track gently down into a wooded valley, then over a gentle rise and down to a road junction. A sign points back to Cova da Roda. Turn left and walk down the cobbled road, which is patched with concrete. It is still wooded, with a tangled undergrowth, but there are cultivated plots along the way too. After crossing a clear-felled area, cross an old levada and walk mostly among pines, to reach another tarmac road at a building. Turn left downhill again, then walk uphill past a stoneworks. Follow the patchy road until it passes a sports pitch and drops to a road junction. Walk down the road, passing a fruit depot and a bar called the Talho a Vaquinha do Norte, to the left. Further downhill, to the right, is the Citradições Pub. Reach a junction with the main ER-101 road, cross over and walk down into the middle of **Santana**. There are places to eat and drink in the village, as well as toilets and a bus stop. There are several little thatched houses, some of them in the classic red and white 'Santana' style colours.

WALK 47: Pico do Suna and Porto da Cruz

There is an interesting walk to Pico do Suna that is mostly downhill. Start on the road from Poiso to Santo da Serra, and indeed some may prefer to walk along this scenic road to reach the start. The walk uses a clear track to reach Pico do Suna, though there is also a detour along a narrow path for fine views. If you want an easy walk then retrace your steps afterwards. The descent to Porto da Cruz starts easily enough but becomes more and more rugged, with some rather narrow, slippery and overgrown paths towards the end. A road-walk completes the descent, then head either for Porto da Cruz or Faial to finish.

THE ROUTE

Distance:
12km (7½ miles).

Start:
On the ER-202 between Poiso and Santo da Serra – 262212.

Finish:
At the church in Porto da Cruz – 292272.

Maps:
Military Survey 1:25,000 Sheet 6 or IGC 1:50,000 Madeira East.

Terrain:
A good track at first on open slopes. More wooded later, with steep and narrow paths that can be rocky or crumbling or overgrown in places.

Start on a bendy stretch of the **ER-202 road** between Poiso and Santo da Serra. A clear and obvious track leaves the road where a sign forbids lighting fires: 'Proibido Fazer Lume'. The track climbs a little, then descends and rises again. There are views eastwards to the Ponta de São Lourenço beyond Santo da Serra. Watch for a narrow path off to the left, flanked by small cairns. It leads up to a lovely ridge of short grass dotted with clumps of heather. Go through a straggly fence and walk along the crest of **Lombo Comprido,** which has three rounded, rocky tops. Enjoy the best views from the last one, taking in the high peaks of Madeira, villages around Faial, steep-sided Penha de Águia, the distant Ponta de São Lourenço and Santo da Serra. If there is a blot on the view, it is a nearby dump. Double back to the previous little gap and turn sharply left along another grassy path to walk down to the track again, and turn left. Heather, bilberry, broom, and laurel flank the track, which heads gently downhill on more densely wooded slopes. Views become limited before a curve to the left and a descent to a gap. A water trough sits on the gap at a junction of tracks.

Take the track on the right to rise quickly to the summit of **Pico do Suna**, where there is a watchtower. If the tower is closed then unfortunately the trees on the summit obscure the views. There is a path leading off the summit that could be used as an alternative descent, leading to the Levada da Portela. If you choose this, then on reaching the levada refer to Walk 6 for a route down to Portela. To continue with the rest of this walk, however, retrace steps to the water trough on the gap and turn sharply right to follow the track further downhill. It is broad at first, but narrows and becomes quite rugged, surrounded by dense 'laurisilva'. It levels out and there are paths to right and left. Do not take them; they lead down to the Levada do Furado, which is in a tunnel beneath the **Cabeço Furado**.

Take care as some parts of the path are narrow and slippery, crumbling in places. The path undulates and goes through a small rock cutting, and there are occasional glimpses of forested ridges, Faial and the sea. The path has a fence to the right, marked as private property, so keep to the left and zig-zag downhill below the forested peak of **Pedreiro**. Pass through tall eucalyptus further downhill. There are a few pines but there was a blaze in the past and eucalyptus colonised the slopes. The path sometimes follows the crest of the ridge or runs on the left side, sometimes zig-zagging more steeply downhill.

At a fork in the path, keep left, then turn right at a junction, taking great care on a crumbling path through gorse and brambles. Some parts are steep and slippery. Mimosa grows in places, and the path is in a rut and partly cobbled. The worst part of the descent is over. Turn left and right along tracks then follow a cobbled track with street lights past houses. A road made of cobbles, concrete and tarmac leads down past two small shops on the way to a road junction at **Cruz**. There is a shop/bar at this point, and there are bus services. Alternatively,

Transport:
Taxi to the start, or walk down the road from Poiso. São Roque Bus 56, 103 and 138 serve Poiso. SAM Bus 53, 56 and 78 serve Porto da Cruz.

Refreshments:
There are small bars at Cruz. There are bars and restaurants at Porto da Cruz.

A view of Madeira's high peaks from the crest of Lombo Comprido

turn left or right to reach Faial or **Porto da Cruz**. Walking down to Porto da Cruz, watch out for a flight of steps and an old road cutting out a loop of road. There are places offering food and drink.

WALK 48: Penha de Águia

THE ROUTE

Distance:
6km (3¾ miles).

Start/Finish:
Bridge over the Ribeira de São Roque do Faial –
274284.

Maps:
Military Survey 1:25,000 Sheet 6 or
IGC 1:50,000 Madeira East.

Terrain:
Steep and narrow steps and paths that can be rocky,
crumbling or overgrown in places. There is plenty of
tree cover on the higher parts.

The relatively small hill called Penha de Águia, or Eagle Rock, looks inaccessible from all sides. The seaward cliff is vertical and a study of the inland flanks suggest that cliffs bar access on all other sides too. There is in fact a narrow path that winds up to the summit from the north-western side of the hill, and this can be coupled with another zig-zag path that descends roughly southwards. A short circular walk can be completed on the hill, but be warned that it can be steep and tiring, and if any of the paths are overgrown, they may prove impassable. This walk is not recommended in wet weather.

Start on the eastern side of the bridge crossing the **Ribeira de São Roque do Faial**. Walk a short way up the road in the direction of Porto da Cruz to see steps rising from the road. Follow these concrete, stone or earth steps steeply uphill. There are street lights alongside and a sheer cliff above. Pass a few pines and malfurada bushes. The path levels out in an area of brambles and divides into three. Take the path on the left to reach a road-end, then follow the road along and gently downhill, passing houses to reach the Restaurante Galé.

Walk up a short flight of steps immediately beside the **restaurant**, then follow a path up through a few cultivation plots. Aim for a whitewashed, red-roofed shed on the hillside, and keep to the left of it. The path is rough and narrow, flanked by brambles, while clumps of heather and malfurada tend to push walkers towards the sea later. Look carefully for the trodden path and crude stone steps, as well as crossing bare rock while climbing the steep and rugged slope. There are splendid views across the bay, and to Faial and the mountains.

The view westwards from Penha de Águia on the rugged ascent

Keep zig-zagging up the path, climbing above old terracing to enter an area covered in pines. The path is narrow and crumbling on a steep slope, and shrubby heather pushes you seawards, as brambles tear at your clothes. Later, the path climbs more easily up a steep slope covered in tall pines, with bracken alongside, but it can be slippery when wet. A swing to the left takes the path up onto a gap on the crest of Penha de Águia. The crest is well defined and undulates gently. There are still plenty of pines but there are also mimosa and eucalyptus trees. Brief views over the edge to the right reveal a sheer cliff. The path is fairly easy, but when it starts climbing again, it is quite narrow. Pick a way uphill using tree roots and stones as footholds. There is a small clearing on the summit of **Penha de Águia**, with most of the space taken by a tall trig point at 589m (1932ft). There are small pines, laurels, heather, gorse, brambles and bilberry around the clearing. There are no sea views; just the villages and mountains lying inland.

A narrow path continues along the crest, descending with views through the trees to the Ponta de São Lourenço and the distant island of Porto Santo. Squeeze past gorse and heather then note how the pines are squeezed out by eucalyptus. The path is narrow and crumbling, leading to a clearing on a gap where a rocky slope falls away to the right. An old winch cable stretches downhill. It is hard to believe, but this is the line of descent, and there is a steep and narrow crumbling zig-zag path. Take great care on this path, which alternates across slopes of grass, shrubs and trees, sometimes on crumbling earth or bare rock. Do not be tempted to short-cut straight downhill, but follow the line of the path faithfully.

When walking past a few mimosa trees, things get better and the path is less steep. There are good coastal views, and although the road can be seen below, care is still needed with the path. There are steep grassy slopes and malfurada bushes, and cultivation terraces on either side. Step a little to the right to find a small levada, then turn left to pass a water tank on the hillside. Walk down through vegetable plots to find steps leading down onto the road. Either turn left to walk down to **Porto da Cruz**, or turn right to complete the circuit by walking back down to the bridge where the walk started. Either way, There is the option of jumping on a bus if one is due, and there are a couple of small bars by the road on the way back to the start.

Transport:
SAM Bus 53, 56 and 78 cross the Ribeira de São Roque do Faial.

Refreshments:
The Restaurante Galé is passed on the ascent. There are small bars by the road towards the end of the walk.

WALK 49: Porto Santo – West and South

The south and western parts of Porto Santo include a huddle of hills, some impressive cliff coast and an amazing sandy beach quite unlike anything else seen in Madeira. The walk is long and takes all day, and coupled with the other walk on Porto Santo, a complete circuit of the island can be made, enjoying all its highlights. The hills are mostly dry and treeless, though on the southernmost slopes you will see how attempts are being made to reforest the dry, stony slopes. Follow this route through the hills, then decide later whether or not to walk along the beach to finish.

THE ROUTE
Distance:
15 or 21km (9½ or 13 miles).
Start:
Camacha.
Finish:
Calheta or Vila Baleira.
Maps:
Plano Director Municipal 1:25,000 Sheet – Porto Santo.
Terrain:
Mostly roads and tracks, with some pathless stretches, crossing dry and stony slopes and cliff edges. The final stretch is along a sandy beach.

Start at the lower end of **Camacha**, following the road signposted for Fonte da Areia. The road runs down alongside the airport fence and swings left to run along the top of a rugged cliff line. A turning on the right is signposted for **Fonte da Areia** and leads down through a cutting in soft calcareous sandstone. The sandstone is a notable source of water, acting as a natural reservoir. There are steps and zig-zag paths leading down to an exotically planted slope and a couple of picnic sites but be careful, do not go too far down as steps have to be retraced back up to the road to continue.

Follow the road further alongside the airport fence, then when the fence turns left, start exploring the desert-like slopes to the left of the road. Note the contrast between the barren bedrock and drifting sand, and the greener parts of the island. Climb to a vantage point and look ahead to spot a fenced enclosure, then walk towards it and keep just to the left. There is a kind of track alongside, but also soft sand, and beware of small quarries further to the left. Reach a clear track that runs along the bedrock, turn left to reach a track junction, then turn right to follow a sandy track up a gentle, green slope. The slope is divided into plots by tumbled walls, but only a few plots are cultivated. Note the abundance of snail shells scattered everywhere. Follow the track uphill and left to reach the highest communications mast on the summit of **Bárbara Gomes**. A trig point stands at 227m (745ft). Not a great height, but views take in the whole island.

To descend, aim well to the right of a stone quarry, then swing left to follow a track along a crest overlooking the sea. The track crosses arid, stony scrub, reaching a gentle gap where it joins a broader track. Bear right to continue. There are good views along the cliff coast, leading the eye to the Ilhéu de Ferro, with the island of Madeira seen beyond. Follow the broad track up to a small building and tall mast on the rounded summit of **Eiras**, where there is a trig point at 176m (577ft). There are views all round the island while passing through a gateway in a tall fence.

A stony track runs downhill, winding past a few bushes, continuing down an arid, stony slope to pass through another gateway in the tall fence. Continue across another broad and gentle gap, then the track begins to drift left inland. (It could be followed to link with a road and quick exit via Campo de Baixo.) Leaving the track, swing right to pass above a rugged cove and face the hill called Espigão. A vague track runs up the slope, and when reaching a higher level, watch for a left turn leading to a dead-end not far from a rocky peak. This is not the highest point, so pick a way along a rocky ridge, which is actually a resistant basalt dyke, leading to the highest point. There is a trig point at 270m (886ft).

Follow the basalt dyke along the crest of **Espigão**. A fence accompanies it, then the fence ends and the dyke peters out at a concrete block. Either continue straight on to descend to a dirt road, or start swinging right, with a little more care, to pick a way down to the dirt road closer to Morenas. (It all depends how much time can be spared. If you are in a hurry, turn left to follow the dirt road.) Turn right along the dirt road and walk down to an exotically

Transport:
Moinho Bus 1 serves Camacha. Moinho Bus 4 serves Calheta.

Refreshments:
There are bars and restaurants at Camacha. The Restaurante Pôr do Sol is at Calheta. There are many bars and restaurants in Vila Baleira.

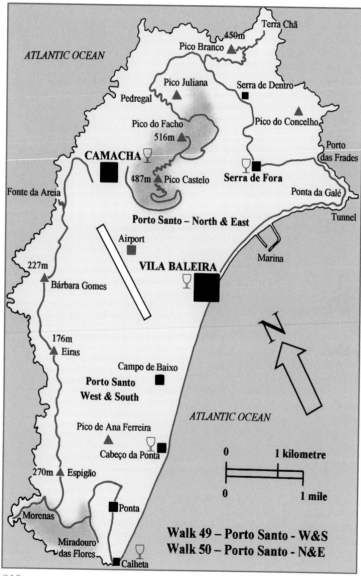

Terra Chã

450m
Pico Branco ▲

ATLANTIC OCEAN

Pico Juliana ▲

Serra de Dentro ■

Pedregal

Pico do Concelho ▲

Pico do Facho
516m ▲

CAMACHA ♓

Porto
das Frades

487m ▲ Pico Castelo

Serra de Fora ■♓

Fonte da Areia

Ponta da Galé

Porto Santo – North & East

Tunnel

Airport ■

Marina

VILA BALEIRA ♓ ■

227m
▲ Bárbara Gomes

N

176m
▲ Eiras

Campo de Baixo ■

**Porto Santo
West & South**

ATLANTIC OCEAN

Pico de Ana Ferreira ▲

Cabeço da Ponta ♓ ■

0   1 kilometre

270m ▲ Espigão

0   1 mile

Morenas

■ Ponta

Walk 49 – Porto Santo - W&S

Miradouro
das Flores

Walk 50 – Porto Santo - N&E

♓ ■ Calheta

planted picnic site at **Morenas**. Pines and prickly pears have been planted on the slopes of Espigão to re-establish vegetation. Follow the track further, out to a parking space and fenced-off viewpoint at Ponta da Canaveira. Take the time to study Ilhéu de Ferro. When it is battered by waves, plumes of spray erupt from one headland.

Retrace steps back along the dirt road, past Morenas, with street lighting alongside while it rises gently. There are pines along both sides of the road for a while on the descent, and there is a track heading off to the left, before a prominent junction of dirt roads. A sign points back to Morenas, and another points right for the **Miradouro das Flores**. The dirt road drops a little, then climbs with street lights alongside, rising above the forested slopes to a car park and viewpoint. A bronze bust of the artist Francisco José Peile da Costa Maya stands here, and the view takes in most of Porto Santo, as well as the Ilhéu de Baixo and the distant island of Madeira.

Walk back down the dirt road, passing the junction for Morenas and another junction for the Adega das Levadas, both to the left. The road runs down to another junction at the foot of Pico de Ana Ferreira, where a turn right is made. Continue straight on past a large building to reach a tarmac road. Either wait here for a bus, or turn left to walk to Cabeço da Ponta and its hotels. To continue with the main walk, however, turn right and keep walking to Calheta.

The road passes buildings old and new, as well as an old limekiln. Walk below the Miradouro das Flores viewpoint and reach the road-end at **Calheta**. The Restaurante Pôr do Sol is available for food and drink, and the bus turns here. Watch the currents in conflict between Calheta and the Ilhéu de Baixo. To follow the beach, simply step down onto the sand and start walking. There is outcropping calcareous sandstone at first, but this dwindles and gives way to vegetated dunes. Turn round the gentle point at **Cabeço da Ponta**, not far from the big Dom Pedro Hotel, though the Luamar Suite Hotel is closer to the beach. There is also access inland to a restaurant and bar. There are floodlights along a stretch of the beach, should anyone be walking late into the

Desert-like dunes near Fonte da Areia and a view of the high hills

night! After an empty stretch of beach, pass the Quinta da Ribeira Salgado, then practically the whole beach is floodlit to the pier at **Vila Baleira**. Flags mark the position of ice cream and drinks cabins. Come ashore at the pier and the Restaurante Esplanada da Praia is immediately to hand. Walking into town, there are many other bars and restaurants offering food and drink.

WALK 50: Porto Santo – North and East

THE ROUTE
Distance:
12, 18 or 25km (7½, 11 or 15 miles).
Start:
Camacha.
Finish:
Camacha, Serra de Fora or Vila Baleira.
Maps:
Plano Director Municipal 1:25,000 Sheet – Porto Santo.
Terrain:
Mostly tracks and paths with some roads, climbing forested and open slopes and sea cliffs. The final stretch is along a coastal track and road.

The northern and eastern parts of Porto Santo include the highest hills on the island, as well as impressive sea cliffs and headlands. The walk is long and takes all day, and coupled with the other walk on Porto Santo, a complete circuit of the island can be made, enjoying all its highlights. Some of the hills are dry and treeless, but there have been laudable attempts to reforest many of the slopes. Follow this route over the highest hills, then decide whether to finish early by returning to Camacha. Either continue to Terra Chã and Serra de Fora to pick up a bus to Vila Baleira, or keep walking round a rugged point to follow a coastal track and road to finish.

Start at the top end of **Camacha**, where a crossroads includes a road signposted for Pico Castelo. This is a quick way to the top, but there is a more leisurely and interesting way. Walk down the road in the direction of Vila Baleira, and the road crosses an old stone-lined levada. It is usually dry and its bed is covered with grass and flowers. Turn left to follow it away from the road, using a clear track alongside. Pass a house and a large dilapidated building. There are grassy terraces above and below the levada, but later the higher slopes are forested. There is a fine view across the airport to the western and southern parts of the island. Feeder channels enter the levada and there are stone step-stiles allowing people to cross at intervals. It is well engineered but it lacks water!

A cobbled road climbs up the slopes of Pico Castelo from Dragoal, near Vila Baleira, and the Capela de Nossa Senhora da Graça is seen across a grassy hollow. Turn left to follow the cobbled road uphill on the higher

215

Vila Baleira, Pico Castelo and Pico do Facho as seen from the sea

forested slopes of the hill. At a junction of cobbled roads, walking straight ahead leads to a descent to Camacha, or reveals a road round the back of Pico Castelo. Turn right, however, to reach a car park, viewpoint and picnic site at the end of the road. Follow a good path downhill a little, passing above a telecommunications building, then a narrow path leads round forested terraces to join a bouldery track climbing more steeply. Look left for a flight of steps, zig-zagging uphill, passing close to a small building and stone benches. There are views along the way and pass the concrete top of a levada-fed tank while zig-zagging further uphill. There is a fine viewpoint planted with flowers around a bronze bust of the Regente Florestal António Schiappa de Azevedo (1870–1926). He was responsible for reforesting Porto Santo's barren hills. This is a better viewpoint than the summit of **Pico Castelo**, which rises a little higher and can be reached by steps. A stone-vaulted building sits on top at 487m (1598ft) but trees block the view.

Walk down steps in the direction of the airport, then turn right and start zig-zagging steeply downhill. Face the higher Pico do Facho as the path drops down to a turning space and picnic site. Walk down a winding track to reach a cobbled road, then turn right to reach a turning point and gateway. A sign to the right indicates a path called the Vereda Pico Castelo Moledo. However, a summit bid can be made by following the dirt road up from the gateway. To do this, climb uphill and turn round a bend and walk on concrete for a short way. Look out for steps on the right, and follow a path between the trees to reach a small building and a tall communications mast. Go behind the building and scramble carefully up bare rock to reach the trig point on the summit of **Pico do Facho** at 516m (1693ft). This is Porto Santo's highest point and there are views all the way round the island. Walk back down to the gateway to continue the walk.

The Vereda Pico Castelo Moledo is a pleasant, grassy path contouring round the slopes of Pico do Facho. It stays on the grassy slopes just below the forest. It is generally clear, sometimes narrow, and undulates gently, zig-zagging uphill at one point before going through a small gateway. Swinging round the slope, plenty of fine hills can be seen, including Pico Juliana, Pico Branco, Pico do Concelho and Pico do Maçarico. Flowers cover the old terraces, leading the eye down to the deserted village of Serra de Dentro. The path enters the forest and winds round the slope to reach a fairly open gap between Pico do Facho and **Pico Juliana**. Walk towards the rocky Pico Juliana by following a crude stone wall, then step left off the ridge and follow a zig-zag stony track down to a road with a picnic site nearby. It is possible to turn left and follow the road back to Camacha in mere minutes, passing the Bar Quinta do Serrado on the way. To walk further, however, then turn right.

The road crosses open slopes, passing a picnic site and viewpoint. There are ruined farms and terraces at **Pedregal**, then a stone works lies ahead. The road zig-zags downhill, though there is a short-cut straight through a bend. A signpost on the left points out the Vereda Terra Chã, which must be one of the least appreciated paths on the island. Walk between short stretches of fencing, climb to another stretch of fencing and turn right. The path climbs gradually across a steep, dry and stony slope. There are a few wooden steps and splendid views back

Transport:
Moinho Bus 1 serves Camacha. Moinho Bus 2 serves Serra de Fora.

Refreshments:
There are bars and restaurants at Camacha. The Restaurante Teodorico and Snack Bar O Volante are at Serra de Fora. There are many bars and restaurants in Vila Baleira.

to Pico Juliana, then walk down a few steps with a fence alongside to turn round a rocky ravine. Follow the path gently up and across the rest of the rugged, open slope. After crossing old terraces, the path has plenty of fencing alongside as it zig-zags steeply uphill, sometimes crossing bare rock. Cross a rocky ridge and suddenly find yourself on a steep slope of pine and cypress. The path has been hacked from the rock.

Turn left at a junction to climb to a fine viewpoint. Stone steps and a zig-zag path lead up a rocky, bouldery, wooded slope to the summit of **Pico Branco**. There is a trig point at 450m (1476ft) and some trees have been felled to open up the view. Walk back downhill, then walk along the other path from the junction. Steps lead down and up, then down and up again. Crunch across red pumice to reach a small building and picnic area at **Terra Chã**. Again there are splendid views of sea cliffs, with terracing in all sorts of unlikely places, as well as more cypress. Turn round and retrace steps all the way back to the road to continue.

Follow the road down to the deserted village of **Serra de Dentro** and see how bad the erosion is, with gullies riven down the hillside. Trees have been planted to stabilise the slopes and dams have been built across the watercourses. Most of the buildings in the village are in ruins, but a handful are inhabited at the bottom of the road. Follow the road up a greener slope, passing a quarry on a gap, then walk down to **Serra de Fora**. Pass a turning for the Restaurante Teodorico, then the road levels out in the village. Not far away is the Snack Bar O Volante, and there are buses to Vila Baleira.

To walk further, turn left along a road signposted for **Porto dos Frades**, which leads down between Pico do Concelho and Pico do Maçarico to a rugged cove. Turn right and follow a track across a streambed where tamarisk bushes grow. A sign warns of falling rocks and the coastal track is subject to constant rockfalls. Pass terraced slopes, then pass through an area of calcareous sandstone. The track enters a big **tunnel** bored through the **Ponta da Galé**, where the island of Ilhéu de Cima can be studied from both sides. Tread with care uphill from

the tunnel as the cliffs above are unstable. In wet weather There is plenty of mud. There is a fine view along the coast on the descent, taking in the Marina, Vila Baleira and the long, sandy beach to Calheta. Join a tarmac road beside a go-kart track and walk past the **marina**. If you see a bus or taxi, then use it to return to **Vila Baleira**. There is also the option of following the beach or the road to reach the town

A quiet cove near Serra de Fora on the walk round the final headland

LISTING OF CICERONE GUIDES

NORTHERN ENGLAND
LONG DISTANCE TRAILS
THE DALES WAY
THE ISLE OF MAN COASTAL PATH
THE PENNINE WAY
THE ALTERNATIVE COAST TO COAST
NORTHERN COAST-TO-COAST WALK
THE RELATIVE HILLS OF BRITAIN
MOUNTAINS ENGLAND & WALES
  VOL 1 WALES. VOL 2 ENGLAND.

CYCLING
BORDER COUNTRY BIKE ROUTES
THE CHESHIRE CYCLE WAY
THE CUMBRIA CYCLE WAY
THE DANUBE CYCLE WAY
LANDS END TO JOHN O'GROATS
  CYCLE GUIDE
ON THE RUFFSTUFF -
  84 Bike Rides in Nth Engl'd
RURAL RIDES No.1 WEST SURREY
RURAL RIDES No.1 EAST SURREY
SOUTH LAKELAND CYCLE RIDES
THE WAY OF ST JAMES
  Le Puy to Santiago - Cyclist's

LAKE DISTRICT AND MORECAMBE BAY
CONISTON COPPER MINES
CUMBRIA WAY & ALLERDALE RAMBLE
THE CHRONICLES OF MILNTHORPE
THE EDEN WAY
FROM FELL AND FIELD
KENDAL - A SOCIAL HISTORY
A LAKE DISTRICT ANGLER''S GUIDE
LAKELAND TOWNS
LAKELAND VILLAGES
LAKELAND PANORAMAS
THE LOST RESORT?
SCRAMBLES IN THE LAKE DISTRICT
MORE SCRAMBLES IN THE
  LAKE DISTRICT
SHORT WALKS IN LAKELAND
  Book 1: SOUTH
  Book 2: NORTH
  Book 3: WEST
ROCKY RAMBLER'S WILD WALKS
RAIN OR SHINE
ROADS AND TRACKS OF THE
  LAKE DISTRICT
THE TARNS OF LAKELAND Vol 1: West
THE TARNS OF LAKELAND Vol 2: East
WALKING ROUND THE LAKES
WALKS SILVERDALE/ARNSIDE
WINTER CLIMBS IN LAKE DISTRICT

NORTH-WEST ENGLAND
WALKING IN CHESHIRE
FAMILY WALKS IN FOREST OF BOW-
  LAND
WALKING IN THE FOREST OF BOW-
  LAND
LANCASTER CANAL WALKS
WALKER'S GUIDE TO LANCASTER

CANAL
CANAL WALKS VOL 1: NORTH
WALKS FROM THE LEEDS-LIVERPOOL
  CANAL
THE RIBBLE WAY
WALKS IN RIBBLE COUNTRY
WALKING IN LANCASHIRE
WALKS ON THE WEST PENNINE
  MOORS
WALKS IN LANCASHIRE WITCH
  COUNTRY
HADRIAN'S WALL
  Vol 1 : The Wall Walk
  Vol 2 : Wall Country Walks

NORTH-EAST ENGLAND
NORTH YORKS MOORS
THE REIVER'S WAY
THE TEESDALE WAY
WALKING IN COUNTY DURHAM
WALKING IN THE NORTH PENNINES
WALKING IN NORTHUMBERLAND
WALKING IN THE WOLDS
WALKS IN THE NORTH YORK MOORS
  Books 1 and 2
WALKS IN THE YORKSHIRE DALES
  Books 1,2 and 3
WALKS IN DALES COUNTRY
WATERFALL WALKS - TEESDALE &
  HIGH PENNINES
THE YORKSHIRE DALES
YORKSHIRE DALES ANGLER'S GUIDE

THE PEAK DISTRICT
STAR FAMILY WALKS PEAK
  DISTRICT/5th YORKS
HIGH PEAK WALKS
WEEKEND WALKS IN THE PEAK DIS-
  TRICT
WHITE PEAK WALKS
  Vol.1 Northern Dales
  Vol.2 Southern Dales
WHITE PEAK WAY
WALKING IN PEAKLAND
WALKING IN SHERWOOD FORES
WALKING IN STAFFORDSHIRE
THE VIKING WAY

WALES AND WELSH BORDERS
ANGLESEY COAST WALKS
ASCENT OF SNOWDON
THE BRECON BEACONS
CLWYD ROCK
HEREFORD & THE WYE VALLEY
HILLWALKING IN SNOWDONIA
HILLWALKING IN WALES Vol.1
HILLWALKING IN WALES Vol.2
LLEYN PENINSULA COASTAL PATH
WALKING OFFA'S DYKE PATH
THE PEMBROKESHIRE COASTAL PATH
THE RIDGES OF SNOWDONIA
SARN HELEN
SCRAMBLES IN SNOWDONIA
SEVERN WALKS
THE SHROPSHIRE HILLS

THE SHROPSHIRE WAY
SPIRIT PATHS OF WALES
WALKING DOWN THE WYE
A WELSH COAST TO COAST WALK
WELSH WINTER CLIMBS

THE MIDLANDS
CANAL WALKS VOL 2: MIDLANDS
THE COTSWOLD WAY
COTSWOLD WALKS Book 1: North
COTSWOLD WALKS Book 2: Central
COTSWOLD WALKS Book 3: South
THE GRAND UNION CANAL WALK
HEART OF ENGLAND WALKS
WALKING IN OXFORDSHIRE
WALKING IN WARWICKSHIRE
WALKING IN WORCESTERSHIRE
WEST MIDLANDS ROCK

SOUTH AND SOUTH-WEST ENGLAND
WALKING IN BEDFORDSHIRE
WALKING IN BUCKINGHAMSHIRE
CHANNEL ISLAND WALKS
CORNISH ROCK
WALKING IN CORNWALL
WALKING IN THE CHILTERNS
WALKING ON DARTMOOR
WALKING IN DEVON
WALKING IN DORSET
CANAL WALKS VOL 3: SOUTH
EXMOOR & THE QUANTOCKS
THE GREATER RIDGEWAY
WALKING IN HAMPSHIRE
THE ISLE OF WIGHT
THE KENNET & AVON WALK
THE LEA VALLEY WALK
LONDON THEME WALKS
THE NORTH DOWNS WAY
THE SOUTH DOWNS WAY
THE ISLES OF SCILLY
THE SOUTHERN COAST TO COAST
SOUTH WEST WAY
  Vol.1 Mineh'd to Penz.
  Vol.2 Penz. to Poole
WALKING IN SOMERSET
WALKING IN SUSSEX
THE THAMES PATH
TWO MOORS WAY
WALKS IN KENT Book 1
WALKS IN KENT Book 2
THE WEALDWAY & VANGUARD WAY

SCOTLAND
WALKING IN THE ISLE OF ARRAN
THE BORDER COUNTRY -
  A WALKERS GUIDE
BORDER COUNTRY CYCLE ROUTES
BORDER PUBS & INNS -
  A WALKERS' GUIDE
CAIRNGORMS, Winter Climbs
  5th Edition

LISTING OF CICERONE GUIDES

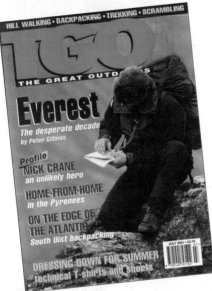

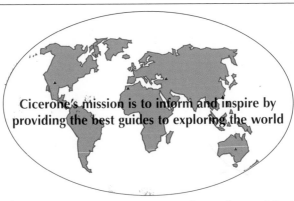

Cicerone's mission is to inform and inspire by
providing the best guides to exploring the world

Since its foundation over 30 years ago, Cicerone has specialised
in publishing guidebooks and has built a reputation for quality
and reliability. It now publishes nearly 300 guides to the major
destinations for outdoor enthusiasts, including Europe, UK and
the rest of the world.

Written by leading and committed specialists, Cicerone guides
are recognised as the most authoritative. They are full of
information, maps and illustrations so that the user can plan
and complete a successful and safe trip or expedition – be it a
long face climb, a walk over Lakeland fells, an alpine traverse, a
Himalayan trek or a ramble in the countryside.

With a thorough introduction to assist planning, clear
diagrams, maps and colour photographs to illustrate the terrain
and route, and accurate and detailed text, Cicerone guides are
designed for ease of use and access to the information.

If the facts on the ground change, or there is any aspect of a
guide that you think we can improve, we are always delighted
to hear from you.

Cicerone Press, 2 Police Square, Milnthorpe, Cumbria LA7 7PY

Tel 01539 562 069   Fax 01539 563 417
email info@cicerone.co.uk   web: www.cicerone.co.uk